Mastering Media with the Raspberry Pi

Media Centers, Music, High End Audio, Video, and Ultimate Movie Nights

Ralph Roberts

Apress®

Mastering Media with the Raspberry Pi: Media Centers, Music, High End Audio, Video, and Ultimate Movie Nights

Ralph Roberts
Alexander, North Carolina, USA

ISBN-13 (pbk): 978-1-4842-2727-5   ISBN-13 (electronic): 978-1-4842-2728-2
https://doi.org/10.1007/978-1-4842-2728-2

Library of Congress Control Number: 2017957568

Cover image designed by Freepik

Managing Director: Welmoed Spahr
Editorial Director: Todd Green
Acquisitions Editor: Natalie Pao
Development Editor: James Markham
Technical Reviewer: Martin V. Minner
Coordinating Editor: Jessica Vakili
Copy Editor: James A. Compton
Compositor: SPi Global
Indexer: SPi Global
Artist: SPi Global

Distributed to the book trade worldwide by Springer Science+Business Media New York, 233 Spring Street, 6th Floor, New York, NY 10013. Phone 1-800-SPRINGER, fax (201) 348-4505, e-mail orders-ny@springer-sbm.com, or visit www.springeronline.com. Apress Media, LLC is a California LLC and the sole member (owner) is Springer Science + Business Media Finance Inc (SSBM Finance Inc). SSBM Finance Inc is a **Delaware** corporation.

For information on translations, please e-mail rights@apress.com, or visit http://www.apress.com/rights-permissions.

Apress titles may be purchased in bulk for academic, corporate, or promotional use. eBook versions and licenses are also available for most titles. For more information, reference our Print and eBook Bulk Sales web page at http://www.apress.com/bulk-sales.

Any source code or other supplementary material referenced by the author in this book is available to readers on GitHub via the book's product page, located at http://www.apress.com/us/book/9781484227275. For more detailed information, please visit http://www.apress.com/source-code.

Printed on acid-free paper

Contents at a Glance

Contents

About the Author

Ralph Roberts is a long-time writer with over 100 books published and more than 20 million words sold professionally (mostly about computers) and the publisher of about 1,000 titles through his own publishing company. He's recently written extensively about the Raspberry Pi—directly coauthoring a book with Eben Upton, founder of the Raspberry Pi Foundation—including thousands of words about its sound and video features. Additionally, he has decades of experience in sound and video, having produced hundreds of hours of TV shows and documentaries. He also owned a small chain of stereo stores and held certification from the Society of Audio Consultants.

CHAPTER 1

■ ■ ■

Which RPi Model Is Right for You?

> *Good things come in small packages.*
>
> —Old saying

The Raspberry Pi (RPi, pronounced R-pi) family of credit-card–sized computer boards certainly comes with many good things in a small package. Literally very close to the length and width of a credit card, albeit thicker, this tiny, powerful computer not only provides many abilities of far larger computers but adds some they do not have.

These include features enabling the mastery of media manipulation we'll learn and utilize in this book, such as the built-in digital-to-analog convertor (DAC); this enables, for one example, conversion of high-quality digital music to analog waveforms to drive headphones or speakers (which are analog devices). The RPi also handles execution of various sound processing, media serving, media storage, and other related tasks with ease.

All that comes soon, but in this chapter we look at the history and various models of the Raspberry Pi and compare their features. In short, you'll see that a surprising amount of computing power, range of input/output protocols and connectivity options, and so on lives on the RPi's board.

First, however, I'll answer the question in the chapter title, "Which RPi model for you?" There are two possible answers, both correct:

1. The one you already have.

2. The latest model. The RPi 3 has four cores, is faster, and has built-in Bluetooth and WiFi, the latter being excellent features to have in a media center.

You may own an earlier model and plan to dedicate it as a media center, or media storage server, or any of the many other media-related uses we'll be exploring in these pages. No problem. Or, since the most recent Raspberry Pi model costs so little (you'll see why that is shortly), you can just buy the latest and greatest. At the time of this writing, that would be the Raspberry Pi 3 for around $35.

© Ralph Roberts 2017
R. Roberts, *Mastering Media with the Raspberry Pi*,
https://doi.org/10.1007/978-1-4842-2728-2_1

These boards cost so little compared to large computers that it's quite feasible to purchase more than one. For instance, you might want a media center, a home security system, or an intelligent controller for any number of other projects. The low cost and high computing power of the Raspberry Pi encourage buying one for each such project and using it permanently. Figure 1-1 shows what an RPi 3 Model B looks like.

Figure 1-1. *The Raspberry Pi 3 Model B is the current model*

So, let's explore the Raspberry Pi in more detail.

A Brief History

The Raspberry Pi came about in a rather unusual manner. We expect most successful technical innovations to birth themselves in the research and development labs of major corporations or, more dramatically, perhaps in the garage of some young geniuses with little money but strong dreams. Steve Jobs and Steve Wozniak creating Apple represent the latter.

Unlike those more conventional scenarios, the inception of RPi resulted from the efforts of a *charity*. The Raspberry Pi Foundation—designers, creators, and owners of the Raspberry Pi—was established in 2009 and duly registered with the Charity Commission for England and Wales.

Supporters of the Foundation included the University of Cambridge Computer Laboratory and Broadcom. The latter, a chip developer and manufacturer, is exceptionally significant to the Raspberry Pi's millions-of-units-sold success. Broadcom supplies the heart of the RPi, its SoC (System on a Chip). We'll explore the SoC later in this chapter (there's a *lot* packed into that tiny chip).

The founders of the Raspberry Pi Foundation included Eben Upton, Rob Mullins, Jack Lang, Alan Mycroft, Pete Lomas, and David Braben. They had realized the need for a small but affordable computer. This information once appeared on the http://raspberrypi.org. About page but has been omitted recently. It's important and reproduced various places on the Internet such as https://elinux.org/RPi_General_History.

"The idea behind a tiny and affordable computer for kids came in 2006, when Eben Upton, Rob Mullins, Jack Lang and Alan Mycroft, based at the University of Cambridge's Computer Laboratory, became concerned about the year-on-year decline in the numbers and skills levels of the A Level students applying to read Computer Science. From a situation in the 1990s where most of the kids applying were coming to interview as experienced hobbyist programmers, the landscape in the 2000s was very different; a typical applicant might only have done a little web design. … Our Foundation's goal is to advance the education of adults and children, particularly in the field of computers, computer science and related subjects."

The About page discusses the decrease in computer literacy among students and declares technology now exists to solve that problem. That technology, of course, is the Raspberry Pi series of inexpensive single-board computers. The RPi, they state, emulates the hands-on appeal of the 1990s "Amigas, BBC Micros, Spectrum ZX and Commodore 64 machines that people of an earlier generation learned to program on."

This resulted in, after several prototypes, the Foundation's release of the Raspberry Pi Model B in 2012 (Figure 1-2). It was an immediate success, selling over 100,000 units in the first day and over two million during the next two years of production.

Figure 1-2. *The Model B had a network port and two USB receptacles. Newer models provide four USB receptacles. (Photo Justin Goetz, Creative Commons).*

In 2014 the Model B+ was released and in 2015, the four-core CPU (Central Processing Unit) Raspberry Pi 2 Model B continued the success. The latter, with greater speed and memory, sold over 500,000 boards in its first two weeks of availability. 2015 also saw the Raspberry Pi Zero—a complete single-board computer for $5—sell out within a short time of release.

The current RPi, the Raspberry Pi 3 Model B, continues the high and still growing popularity. We'll look at the differences in these models later in this chapter.

One more impetus to the RPi's amazing success remains. Adults! Yes, the Pi was developed for kids, and students in schools all over the world continue to learn and be inspired by it. However, we adults—especially various hobbyists—almost immediately saw the wonder and incredible *usefulness* of a powerful computer small enough to run off batteries and be put *anywhere*. Model aircraft, ham radio, listening to music, watching video—you name the hobby or more serious application like security systems—this tiny but super single-board computer finds wide usage.

A Tasty Slice of Pi

The Raspberry Pi's greatest excitement for users comes from its *density*. All sorts of computer power strains to get out from this small board.

How does it compare with a desktop PC or laptop? Well, the RPi does not have a built-in power supply or fancy displays or big hard drives or massive amounts of memory like PCs. However, you can add peripherals to it and achieve all sorts of good stuff. Attach large hard drives, 60-inch HDMI screens, high-end sound systems, 50-page-per-minute laser printers, and much more.

Advantages

Following are five of the major advantages the Raspberry Pi enjoys over large computers. These apply to all models but, again, buying the latest model is always the best choice in taking advantage of improved performance and features:

1. At around $35 retail, it's very inexpensive.

2. Its exceptionally compact, credit-card sized form makes it easy to embed into projects.

3. You can put in a totally different operating system in seconds by inserting a new SD (Secure Digital) or microSD card for almost instant reconfiguration and repurposing.

4. The RPi, thanks to its SoC, has more interfaces, communications protocols, and other features out of the box than conventional computers selling for many times its cost.

5. The GPIO (General Purpose Input/Out) pins allow programmable control of real world-devices.

Basically, the RPi works like a normal computer but at a considerably lower cost. It can even be used as a web or other server. While it may not have the memory and storage of larger servers, you can achieve that by grouping Raspberry Pi boards together. Building a parallel-processing server or even a supercomputer array out of RPi units has been done and is certainly cost effective over purchasing big, fancy servers for thousands of dollars each.

And, for the purposes of this book, a huge advantage of the RPi is the ease with which it can control and play high-end music, show HD video, and do all sorts of sound and other media processing. It even comes with an HDMI output to directly drive our fancy flat-screen TVs hanging on the wall.

Uses

Many uses exist for the Raspberry Pi, but a major one encompasses all sorts of entertainment. For the purpose of this book, the focus includes high-quality digital music as well as movies. A number of interesting extensions in both hardware and software provide us with exciting options.

For example, the HiFiBerry Amp+, shown in Figure 1-3, plugs into the top of all RPi boards after the first Model B. This type of board is called a "tophat" board and pugs into the RPi's GPIO pins and is kept stable with simple spacers, screws, and washers.

Figure 1-3. *Inexpensive 25-watt-per-channel stereo amplifier made specifically for the Raspberry Piasd*

The HiFiBerry products are made and marketed by an independent company. The Amp+ in Figure 1-3 converts digital music and other sound files or streams to analog sound and outputs it through its built-in 25-watt-per-channel amplifier. Insert this board onto the top of your RPi, attach it with the supplied hardware, hook up two speakers, and add a small power supply that drives both the amp and the Raspberry Pi, and you'll fill the room with amazing quality sound.

I bought the one in Figure 1-3 to experiment with for a previous book. It wound up becoming part of my permanent home media center, the one we share construction of during this book. Love it.

SoC, the Sweet Secret of Success

What make the Raspberry Pi and other tiny single-board computers possible is the SoC. This integrated circuit allows placing of the CPU(s), GPU (Graphics Processing Unit), and all sorts of other digital, analog, or mixed-signal circuits in one smaller-than-your-thumb package.

Earlier models of the RPi have the Broadcom BCM2835, and the Raspberry Pi 2 a BCM2636 (a major difference being a single CPU in the first chip and four-cores in the BCM2836). The newest RPi, the Raspberry Pi 3, sports the BCM2837 chip as shown in Figure 1-4.

Figure 1-4. *The Broadcom System on a Chip is the heart of the Raspberry Pi*

Features and Services

The SoC constitutes a major innovation in computing. That is the replacement of many larger components by putting them into a small integrated circuit, thus dramatically reducing physical space requirements. This density of circuitry, again, makes a powerful yet credit-card-sized computer possible, which brings us to the latest and greatest SoC for the RPi, the Broadcom BCM2837. This chip was specially designed by Broadcom for the Raspberry Pi 3. It has more speed, more memory, on-board WiFi, and Bluetooth, and more.

Nice stuff, but some people don't get past the more speed, more memory thing. An even more important addition to the Raspberry Pi 3 is wireless radio. This allows Bluetooth and WiFi (wireless network) communications. Although controlled via the SoC, the radio resides in a tiny (as in *really* small) chip also made by Broadcom, the BCM43438. This chip enables both transmit and receive functions for communicating with wireless access points.

Why, in a media-oriented book, would we care about wireless capability? Because of Bluetooth speakers and headphones, and the ease of pulling in media from our local network or even streaming music and videos off the web.

The Raspberry Pi Family

Millions of Raspberry Pi boards are out there. Table 1-1 introduces this family of single-board computers and shows the differences between them.

Table 1-1. *Raspberry Pi Family*

Model	Release	CPU	Memory	Price
Model A	Feb. 2012	1 × 700MHz	256MB	US$25
Model A+	Nov. 2014	1 × 700MHz	512MB	US$20
Model B	Apr. 2012	1 × 700MHz	512MB	US$35
Model B+	Jul. 2014	1 × 700MHz	512MB	US$25
RPi 2 Model B	Feb. 2015	4 × 900MHz	1GB	US$35
RPi 3 Model B	Feb. 2016	4 × 1.2GHz	1GB	US$35

The Raspberry Pi 3 Model B is preferred for the purposes of this book.

Now let's move on to looking at the ways of powering our Raspberry Pi boards in the next chapter.

CHAPTER 2

■ ■ ■

Power

Electricity is really just organized lightning.

—George Carlin

Let's look at all the ways of powering the Raspberry Pi and its associated devices, including batteries for making it portable or running it in your car or other vehicle. Batteries may even provide power for control functions on board a quadcopter or some other type of radio-controlled model aircraft. And—not surprisingly considering the topic of this book—powering the RPi and associated devices enables making your music and video truly portable.

Or not. Even if we're building a home entertainment center that remains in one place, it's important to know the power requirements of the Raspberry Pi. So, yes, we're getting a little technical here but it's all simple stuff like using Ohm's Law to calculate current and wattage requirements, using a multimeter, and other power-related stuff you'll understand after this chapter. Avoid burning out just one $35 RPi, and this chapter has paid for itself.

Power Basics

Some folks mistake voltage for power. It is not. A *volt*—named in honor of the Italian physicist Alessandro Volta (1745-1827)—measures electromotive force. That's the potential for current to move (be drawn) through an electronic circuit.

This section looks at the basic parameters of electricity—the volt, amp, ohm, and watt. They all work together in creating power. We'll see how they interact and learn their uses.

The Raspberry Pi (all models so far—A, B, and B+, 2, and 3) use a microUSB plug to receive power.

© Ralph Roberts 2017
R. Roberts, *Mastering Media with the Raspberry Pi*,
https://doi.org/10.1007/978-1-4842-2728-2_2

Figure 2-1 is a view of the power connector, this one on a Raspberry Pi 3.

Figure 2-1. *The microUSB power connector on a Raspberry Pi 3*

The microUSB has been around awhile. In 2007 the USB-IF (USB Implementers' Forum)—the folks setting standards for USB connectors—released the current specs. Being tiny, this connector was snapped up by many phone manufacturers and others making small devices with limited space. Zillions of smartphones today (excluding the iPhone for some reason known only to Apple) use the microUSB as a charging port.

The designers of the Raspberry Pi chose it for several good reasons, some of which are:

- It's small and takes up hardly any space.

- Because so many device manufacturers use the microUSB, it is cheap.

- And because its use is so widespread, cords and power supplies are plentiful.

That last bullet point has a potential problem for us. Not all devices require as much power as the Raspberry Pi does. The Model B needs 1 amp, and Model B+ and RPi 2 require about 2 amps. The RPi 3 needs 2.5 amps. These values, by the way, are not set in stone. A 2.4 amp or slightly less adapter might run a Raspberry Pi Model 3 OK—depends on the number of peripherals attached and so forth.

In choosing a power source for your RPi, a wall unit is best and I strongly recommend that choice (Figure 2-2). You can, of course, use a cable like the one that came with your smartphone (microUSB on one and end and standard USB on the other; they are widely available) and just plug it into your computer. However, be forewarned that USB circuits on PCs and other computers have their own power requirements. There might be times when there's not enough current for the RPi to perform properly.

Figure 2-2. *A 2.5 amp wall adapter for Raspberry Pi 3*

Like most of us who have many gadgets (and love them), I have several little power supplies for phones, cameras, and so on scattered around. Many of them might look large enough to run your Raspberry Pi, but check them by reading the voltage and current on the plug.

Or, because they're cheap, you can just buy one. When purchasing a USB charger/ power adapter, make sure it has at least 1 amp current out for a Model B, 2 amps out for a Model B+ and RPi 2, and 2.5 amps out for the RPi 3. Greater current capacity never hurts, either. Figure 2-3 shows what ratings to look for.

Figure 2-3. *Volatage and current ratings are on adapters as shown here*

The critical information in determining whether a wall adapter will run your Raspberry Pi is the Output line. It should be 5 volts (that what the RPi must have) and sufficient current to run your RPi. The one in Figure 2-3 came with one of my Raspberry Pi 3 boards and it has 2.5 amps. In short, the adapter should be very close to the rating. Slightly less may work. Anything above it is OK. A 5 amp adapter, for example, will work just as well as a 2.5 amp since the RPi draws only what it needs.

Most of these adapters sell for under $10.

Use What You've Got

You can just look for any old power supplies (phone chargers, and so on) either locally or online. Check the current rating: 5 V DC at 1 A for the Model B and 5 V DC at 2 A for the Model B+ or the RPi2, with a microUSB connector, like the one pictured in Figure 2-4.

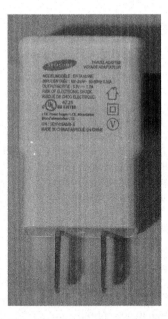

Figure 2-4. *One of my old phone chargers provides 2 A and has been runnng my RPi 2 for over a year now*

By the way, the suggested voltage range on the Raspberry Pi official website is between 4.75 and 5.25 V DC. The adapter in Figure 2-4 is 5.3 V DC but has run my RPi 2 without problems. Still, it's better to stay within the published range.

Buying Online

Purchasing your replacement, should you not find a usable one around your house or office, is easy. Just open your browser to Amazon.com, and a drone taps at your window with the order before you can even enter it. Well, maybe not quite that fast (but it's coming). Still, there's a much greater selection of just about anything you need with fast delivery.

Let me say here that Amazon is an example only because they rather dominate online ordering. Plenty of other places exist where we can buy stuff using the World Wide Web. In addition, do not forget, eBay offers all sorts of both new and used items.

The problem is that they all will send you whatever you order—even if it's wrong. Check specifications before you order.

How do you make sure it's the correct power supply? Look at the specs; they present you with information something like this, usually in somewhat tiny type:

- Input: 100 - 240 VAC

- Output: 5.1V DC / 1A Regulated

- Micro USB Plug

- 5ft Cord Length

- UL Listed

OK, cool. That's good; it will work on the wall voltages in both the U.S. and other countries—the US is 110 volts AC and Europe is 220.The output voltage, 5.1 V DC is OK to run the Raspberry Pi.

The current, 1 A, means it's good to go for powering a Model B. Go back to your search list if you need the power supply to run a B+, RPi 2, or RPi 3 (2A, 2A, 2.5A respectively).

The cord length's fine—unless you need a longer cord, in such case keep searching.

"UL Listed" we've seen on electrical devices and appliances all our lives (since 1894 and in over 40 countries now). It means the device was tested and approved by Underwriters Laboratories and has their stamp of approval—certainly doesn't hurt to have that.

The second method merely requires you to search Amazon (or any other electronic parts vendor online). Use the search term "raspberry pi power supply" (no need for capitalization).

Checking the specs for a typical adapter, we might see:

- Input: AC 110-250 V 0.15 A 50/60Hz.

- Output: DC 5 V 2000 mA (2A). 2000mA is enough to power both your Raspberry Pi and USB devices.

- Suitable for international use.

- Short circuit/overload protection.

- US 2-pin plug.

- Manufactured specifically for the Raspberry Pi.

- CE certified.

2000 mA or milliamps is 2 A (dividing by 1,000 converts milliamps to amps). That power supply would be fine for B+ and Raspberry Pi 2, or even the older Model B if you want a lot of headroom. Do not worry about the input current being so much less; the power is what counts, and power (Ohm's Law) is current times voltage: 0.15 amps times 110 is 16.5 watts and (after being converted from 110 V AC to 5 V DC, 5 times 2 A = 10 watts (the rest is loss due to inefficiency and shows up as heat, which is why adapters are warm under load).

Input voltage is good for United States. or Europe (or just about any other country in the world with adapter plugs). It has 2000 mA current rating, which converts to 2 A, enough current to run a B+.

It's suitable for international use and provides short circuit/overload protection, good features to have.

The US 2 pin plug means we can slide it into our wall sockets and it will work.

Ah, "manufactured specifically for the Raspberry Pi" is nice to know.

On the last point, the letters *CE* are an abbreviation of the French "Conformité Européene," or "European Conformity." This just means the product is OK for sale in the European Community.

Therefore, we've done our due diligence (checked things out) and found a Raspberry Pi-specific power supply, as shown in Figure 2-5.

Figure 2-5. *This power supply was included with my most recent purchase of a Raspberry Pi 3 and is designed specifically for that board*

Using What You Have

However, what if you need a power supply right now, like this very minute? Even with fast shipping from the online vendors, there's no time to waste.

Well, here's another beauty of our modern age. Most of us have devices that use USB charging cables with the wall units in drawers or boxes or otherwise spread around our homes and offices or (for you students) cluttering up your locker at school. Yes, I kept electronic stuff in my locker.

Especially if you have had several years' worth of smartphones (at least the Android types), there are several chargers no longer in use. Sorry, iPhone cables have those weird connectors.

Here's how you make sure a power supply you already have will work.

1. Does it have a microUSB connector? Yes, continue.

2. Check the specs in that tiny little print? 5 V DC. Yes, continue.

3. 1 A for a B or 2 A for a B+ or RPi 2? Or 2.5 A for the RPi 3? Yes, continue.

4. Does it work? Well, plug it in the wall and into the RPi. Red light? It works.

Repurposing power supplies you already have probably should be the first thing you try. It saves you money and time. As you see by now, finding proper power supplies for your RPi requires little effort if you know the specs.

Additional Power

OK, let's look at power a different way. So far this chapter has concerned getting power *into* the Raspberry Pi. Now we flip that around and discuss taking power *out* of the RPi.

Most commonly, we get power out via the USB receptacles. The earlier RPi models had only two but the later models give us four.

The immediate temptation here is to hang all sorts of USB-powered peripherals in, just as we do on desktop or laptop computers—a keyboard, mouse, sound card, and hard drive. Heck, maybe even one of those USB heat pads to keep our coffee warm.

Don't. Or at least not until I show you how. The Raspberry Pi's small form can't provide that kind of power out directly. Indirectly is another matter.

Here's a quick example of exactly what "power out" means. The RPi 3 draws a total of 2.5 A. Of this current, 1.2 A is allocated to the four USB receptacles. Divide that amount by four and each receptacle has on 400 mA or 0.4 A to spend on powering anything plugged into it.

Here's the disadvantage in that. Using a Raspberry Pi as a media server, for instance, serving up music and video requires lots of storage space (media files, especially video) tend to be large.

In my case, I've got some nice USB-powered 1 TB (Terabyte) portable hard drives full of movies and other videos. Be nice to have two or three of those attached to my RPi media center. One of those drives is on the desk here as I write this. Picking it up and reading the power requirements reveals 1 A of current just for that one drive (Figure 2-6).

Figure 2-6. This 1TB portable hard drive requires 1.0 A as shown on its label

The RPi 3 running my media center has, as we saw earlier, only 1.2 A total. So just hooking up one drive leaves only 200 mA for all three of the remaining receptacles. Not good. Other peripherals are needed as well.

Our solution is a *powered* USB hub. That's a USB unit with several receptacles and a power supply that plugs into the wall or some external power supply with more available current than the Raspberry Pi. Run a USB cord from the hub to the Pi and let the hub provide power for the hard drives, and so on

There are still some things you should know, however. First of all, the USB 2.0 standard, such as provided by the Raspberry Pi, only allows for a total of 500 mA per receptacle. The newer USB 3.0 standard (which communicates with the Pi acceptably) added current capacity per receptacle but only bringing it up to 900 mA. Still a bit short for my 1 A portable drives.

However, the USB 3.0 standard recently added a BC.2 protocol for charging ports. Up to 5 amps. Problem solved.

There are several powered hub choices out there. I suggest you look for one that's been tested with the Raspberry Pi. There's an online list of tested hubs for the RPi at http://elinux.org/RPi_Powered_USB_Hubs.

I, however, chose one not recommended but which solves my HD problem, the Plugable (that's the brand name) 7-port USB 3.0 hub, a 25 W powered USB hub with two BC 1.2 charging ports. It's about $30 from various online retailers.

It's not recommended by the manufacturer for RPi usage, because the Raspberry Pi does not yet support the USB 3.0 standard, and some devices (keyboards being one) do not work. However, with four USB receptacles on the RPi 2 and 3, that's not a problem for me. So in choosing a powered hub, look at the current requirement for each of the peripherals you'll be plugging into your media controller (the RPi) and select a hub that has USB receptacles with sufficient current to power them. For example, a hard drive like mine in Figure 2-6 would need a receptacle that could supply 1 A.

Figure 2-7 shows the Plugable hub I have.

Figure 2-7. *A powered USB hub*

One other consideration in choosing a powered hub is *backfeeding*. Backfeeding means hooking a USB cord from a regular port on the hub to a port (receptacle is the correct term) on the RPi and the RPi powers up. This is not good because it bypasses the voltage regulation circuits on the Raspberry Pi board and a power surge could cause damage to the Pi.

The tested hubs on the eLinux site and the Plugable hub I have do not backfeed. It's best to run the RPi from its own power connection and *not* through the hub at all. This lets the hub supply an additional 2.5 A of external power by not having to give that to the Pi (in the case of the RPi 3).

Having a powered hub, then, allows connecting all sorts of additional USB devices. Should you need even more power, merely add another powered hub, connecting it to the RPi.

What We Learned

In this chapter, we delved into power sources for all the Raspberry Pi models.

We saw the easy to use calculations with formulas provided by Ohm's Law. We considered the necessary parameters for choosing a wall-socket power supply for the RPi. We also learned that USB circuits on a PC or Mac might not be reliable (depending on load) and that the wall unit's more reliable.

The rules for choosing RPi power supplies were noted, and we jumped into portable power supplies of all sorts. We found the UBEC (Universal Battery Eliminator Circuit) to be very fine in letting us get 5 V DC for the Pi out of a wide range of batteries, use in automobiles, and powering up with solar chargers. We also received an introduction to power out using powered USB hubs.

Next we move on to storage devices for the Raspberry Pi. As you no doubt already know, music and video requires plenty of storage space. How much storage space? Well, "not enough" is far easier to achieve than "too much."

CHAPTER 3

■ ■ ■

Storage

Back up my hard drive? How do I put it in reverse?

—Unknown

Program and data storage makes a computer useful, but tons of music and video make it rock! That's what we're all about in this book, *entertainment*.

The reality of our need for diversion is that the more we do, the more storage we need. Digital music files require megabytes of space and movies in the gigabytes. The higher the quality (and we want our quality), the bigger the file. So, this chapter shows you the available starting point—what the Raspberry Pi comes standard with—and how we use this beginning to expand into the gigabytes and terabytes for which we yearn.

The RPi's ready for this and soon you will be, too. We'll look first at working memory.

Working Memory

Most of us know by now that computers, and that certainly include the Raspberry Pi, have two kinds of memory. We call those *working memory* and *storage*.

Speaking of storage, SD and microSD cards usually won't really have enough of that for an entertainment center. Movies, for example, can take several gigabytes each. Multiply that by, say 200 movies, and memory cards get left in the dust. However, I guarantee, we will have a grand old time adding vast amounts of storage by attaching hard disks. Later in this chapter, I will show you my RPi 3 that has over 5TB (terabytes) of storage space. It's easy to do.

First, however, we look at the memory space where all programs run, the working memory.

Working memory pulls in programs and data from storage or other inputs. It runs the programs, most often several at a time, and generates more data. Our software records the results we want to keep onto the memory storage device.

When we power down an RPi or it otherwise loses power, working memory erases itself with nothing retained.

We refer to working memory (memory that only works when power is present) as volatile memory and as RAM (Random Access Memory). Volatile memory costs less and runs programs faster. That is the reason for its use.

© Ralph Roberts 2017
R. Roberts, *Mastering Media with the Raspberry Pi*,
https://doi.org/10.1007/978-1-4842-2728-2_3

Storage memory, as on an SD card or a hard drive, offers far more capacity but is slower. It takes time in reading data or programs from the storage memory and/or recording data onto it.

Operating Systems and Processes

Each time the board receives power after a shutdown, the system loads the routines needed to boot up (load in the operating system) into the working memory. These boot-up programs reside on the storage media—SD card or hard drive or, often, on some sort of ROM (Read-Only Memory) chip, which retains its memory even when power is off.

A boot-up process starts when power comes on and the operating system loads and begins operation. Several programs run in the background all the time; we call them *processes*.

Processes run stuff. They handle tasks like recognizing when we hook a keyboard to a USB port or a network presents itself. Usually several dozen of these housekeeping programs buzz along merrily at any one time. It's all part of the magic that makes any computer a computer.

The working memory hosts everything the board actively does. Most Model B boards and all B+ sport 512MB (megabytes or millions of bytes). That may sound like a lot, but you will find several applications requiring more. The RPi 2 and RPi 3 double RAM to 1GB (a *gigabyte* or 1,000 megabytes).

One such application is to employ the RPi as an Internet server of some type. Servers run many concurrent processes and eat up RAM. This slows your board down and can even cause it to lock up (often called "freezing").

Because some applications require a lot of memory, you should always keep in mind proper management of memory resources. Techniques for that require a little programming, which we will look at as needed.

Following are some types of servers you might want run on an RPi (often more than one of these simultaneously):

- Web server: Serves up web pages.

- Mail server: Receives and sends email.

- File server: Provides a place to store and retrieve files from over a network.

- Name server: Provides DNS (dynamic name services) to a network so that when you type a URL (Universal Resource Locator), this looks up the actual Internet protocol (IP) address of the site you want.

- Game server: Lets video game clients connect so that you and your friends can play together online.

- Database server: Used for storing and retrieving large amounts of data.

- Print server: Connects computers over a network to printers.

- Sound server: Streams multimedia broadcasting—music, movies, TV shows over your network.

- Video server: Acquires and streams video to an HDTV or other viewing device.

All of those and more, the RPi does. However, as already mentioned, these uses surely will call for more memory than comes standard on the Pi (with the current model, the RPi 3, 1GB).

The problem that prevents us from simply adding more RAM to a Raspberry Pi involves the compact design and construction of the board, in which working memory is a chip stacked underneath the central processing unit (CPU).

This design prevents up from us plugging in an additional memory board. A simple way around that limitation involves using a swap file for additional memory.

To sum up this section:

- The Raspberry Pi has two types of memory—working (RAM) and storage (SD or microSD card and attached device such as a hard drive).

- Working memory or RAM is volatile, meaning that whenever the board shuts down, everything in the memory erases.

- We cannot easily increase the working memory, because of the compactness of the board's design.

- We can add a swap file to virtually increase working memory by devoting a portion of a hard drive to it (using the SD card is not recommended).

- Because the RPi runs many processes in the background and RAM is limited, memory management is important.

Now that working memory has been introduced, we can move to somewhere a bit roomier, storage memory. First, we look at is the basic memory storage device used by the Raspberry Pi, the SD and/or microSD card.

Card Tricks

The original Model B supports SD cards, while the new B+, RPi 2, and RPi 3 use the smaller microSD card. Note the difference in size in Figure 3-1.

Figure 3-1. *Standard SD and MicroSD cards*

Backward from what you might think, newer microSD cards work in the old Model B. However, the Model B+ cannot read the older SD cards (they are way too big physically). Figure 3-2 shows a microSD-to-SD adapter.

Figure 3-2. *Adaptor for using microSD cards in SD readers*

Creating Cards

What this incompatibility means to you is both good and bad, but there are ways of resolving the problem.

The good is that anything on a card created on a Model B+ runs fine in a Model B and above—assuming software is compatible and as long as you have the adapter shown earlier. This adapter often comes in the package when you purchase a microUSB card, so it is plentiful.

The bad? Not all that great stuff you might have on SD cards will work on the B+ without a bit of effort. We'll make that effort just a bit later in this chapter.

Where do we start? The NOOBS Card is the easiest entry point for getting your RPi up and running.

The NOOBS Card Revisited

NOOBS, according to the Raspberry Pi Foundation, means "New Out Of the Box Software." We could construe NOOBS as a play on the term *newbies*, meaning someone new to a field. That's often somewhat of an insult. However, I won't use it that way here. By this time, we're way ahead of the people who don't even know what a Raspberry Pi is.

Which reminds me—the other day someone asked what I was working on these days? "A book about the Raspberry Pi," I answered.

"What do you know about cooking," he said with a laugh.

Well, I did write a bestselling cookbook once, so I knew more about recipes than he did concerning powerful credit-card-sized computers.

The point being, this bus has no newbies on it. This far into the book, I know you know at least something about the Raspberry Pi. However, we can still benefit from the NOOBS card.

It lets us try out various operating systems and find the best one for a specific project.

The NOOBS card itself is a shortcut. It's an SD or, now also, a microSD card, already formatted and ready to use. On it, we find these six operating systems:

- Raspbian: A port (converted and optimized to run on the RPi) of the popular Debian Wheezy Linux distribution, it is recommended by the Raspberry Pi Foundation, many thousands of other experiments, and me as the best operating system for the RPi.

- Linux: An RPi version for Arch Linux design to run on ARM central processor chips (named after the company that developed it) using RISC (Reduced Instruction Set Computing), which is a way of using fewer processor cycles for greater efficiency on small, limited-resource computers.

- Pidora: A version of Red Hat's Fedora Linux distribution.

- OpenELEC: A dedicated media center distribution.

- RaspBMC: A media center distribution based on Raspbian.

- RISC OS: A non-Linux/Unix-based system.

The best use of the NOOBS card, as mentioned earlier, is in trying out systems. The NOOBS card presents you with six of the most popular ones.

That might be enough, but literally dozens of other operating systems for the RPi can be yours for a free download.

Speaking of free downloads; you could buy the NOOBS card on Amazon, eBay, the Raspberry Pi's own Swag Store, or from any number of other vendors on the web. However, with a bit of that extra effort alluded to, you can download it (or individual operating systems) free from the official Raspberry Pi site (`http:// raspberrypi.org`).

The extra effort means you download a .zip compressed file and use that to build an SD or microSD card. We'll do that next.

Making A NOOBS or Other Operating System Card

Okay, we save a few bucks by downloading and making our own NOOBS card.
It's easy.

We start with the simplified procedure for Windows. You'll need:

1. A computer with an SD slot or external USB media card reader

2. An SD or microSD card, depending on whether you have a Model B or one of the later Raspberry Pi models

3. A small program to write the image file (not a picture but the complete file system) to the SD or microSD card

On the web, go to https://www.raspberrypi.org/downloads/ and you'll see NOOBS on the top section of the page (Figure 3-3).

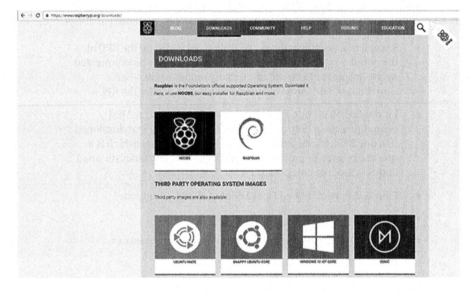

Figure 3-3. *Download NOOBS*

Further down the page is a selection of individual operation systems. The same procedure we use to make a NOOBS card—that is, making a card with only one operating system on it—applies to any of these as well. There are more than shown here; scroll down to see them.

Download NOOBS and/or any of the third-party operating systems you want to turn into SD or microSC cards. I definitely recommend Raspbian. As stated before, it's the most popular operating system on the RPi and used in many of the projects you'll encounter here and elsewhere.

In this book, however, we'll be using the customized Linux-based operating system bundled with the Kodi media center software. This versatile program words best with an optimized version of Linux. We'll discuss that later on.

To repeat a bit of what we discussed in Chapter 1, one of the Raspberry Pi's major advantages is these tiny cards. To switch complete operating systems is a matter of a few seconds. Just do the following:

1. Power off the RPi.

2. Switch the current card with one that has a completely different system.

3. Return power to the RPi board.

This trick is not available on conventional desktops, laptops, pads, smartphones, and so on It can take hours to change the operating system on those and going back to the previous system with whatever files you had in it is often impossible or at least a major pain.

I suggest downloading three of the images from the official Raspberry Pi site via the link given at the top of this section:

1. NOOBS (lets you play with several systems)

2. Raspbian (the most used operating system on the Raspberry Pi)

3. OSMC (one of several open source media centers we look at in later chapters)

Downloading the image of an entire operating/file system takes time. The NOOBS download, for example is a hefty 1.1 GB and that's in compressed format, a `.zip` file, which shortens download time. The first two files in the list will be in zipped format.

To extract the compressed zip file (under Windows), right-click on the compressed file and choose Extract from the dropdown list. A subdirectory is created and you'll find the uncompressed image there.

OSMC is in a `.gz` file, a type of compressed file found most often in Linux operating systems. Get 7-Zip, also open source and a utility that will decompress `.gz` and many other types of files. It's at `http://www.7-zip.org/`.

Once you've downloaded and unpacked one or more of these images to a hard drive, you have image files as shown in Figure 3-4.

Name	Date modified	Type	Size
NOOBS_v2_1_0	12/11/2016 11:43 ...	File folder	
OSMC_TGT_rbp2_20161128.img	12/11/2016 9:51 PM	File folder	
2016-11-25-raspbian-jessie.zip	12/12/2016 12:18 ...	Compressed (zipp...	1,504,184 KB
NOOBS_v2_1_0.zip	12/11/2016 10:14 ...	Compressed (zipp...	1,146,957 KB
OSMC_TGT_rbp2_20161128.img.gz	12/11/2016 9:46 PM	GZ File	160,292 KB

Figure 3-4. *Downloaded image files*

Burning Images to SD/microSD cards

Now that we have an image ready to create an operating system on a card for a Raspberry Pi, we need only one other small piece of utility software, an image burner. While the later versions of Windows (7 and 10) possess built-in image burning capabilities, these only work with CDs and DVDs. On the official Raspberry Pi site, they recommend Win32 Disk Imager. Get it at https://sourceforge.net/projects/win32diskimager/ and install.

NOOBS

Let's set up NOOBS first.

At this point, it's worth emphasizing again the ease of switching SD or microSD cards on the RPi. You can have a whole handful of these relatively inexpensive little memory cards, changing them out as required.

Moving NOOBS to a memory card, by the way, is different than installing an .iso image (as we do for most operating systems). In this instance, we just copy files. This is because NOOBS downloads other files from the Internet to install operating system.

Here we go.

1. Insert the new card (or an old one that can be erased) into the SD reader on or attached to your computer.

2. Go to the directory where you unzipped the files after downloading NOOBS.

3. Format the SD card if needed.

4. Copy all the files in the extracted NOOBS folder to the SD card.

5. Eject the card and insert it into your powered down Raspberry Pi.

6. Power up the RPi and follow the prompts.

Simple, but now we'll burn a complete operating system .iso. It's not much harder but we'll need that special piece of software downloaded earlier, the Win32DiskImager package.

Transferring Operating System Images

NOOBS exists for trying out different operating systems. If you know what you want, then burning the image file of the compete OS/file system to the SD or microSD is the only way to go. The steps for accomplishing this task follow:

1. Insert the memory card into the card reader on your computer. No formatting is required since everything on the card will be written over.

2. Determine the drive number of the card, such as **G:**, for example. Be sure, because having the wrong drive could damage data on other drives during the burning process.

3. Run Win32DiskImager and select the `.iso` file unzipped from the download separate operating system `.zip` file.

4. Select the drive letter of the card reader (see step 2).

5. Select Write and wait until the process completes.

6. Exit Win32DiskImager and eject the card.

You are now ready to insert the card into the Raspberry Pi and boot up into your new operating system.

Converting SD to microSD Cards

The Model B was the last RPi that used SD cards. From the Raspberry Pi B+ on, the standard has been microUSB cards. In the event you have an older model but want to use all or part (data or programs) of the SD card on your newer board, two possibilities exist:

1. It will work.

2. Some of it might work.

The first case comes about because the later models have upgraded their capacities and thus likely call for the latest version of Raspbian or whatever operating system is in use. So update the OS on the SD card before bringing it to your PC for conversion.

In the second case, if the operating system won't boot the new RPi, we can still pull off programs and data and transfer those. Here are the two methods. The first way is by converting an SD card to a microSD card:

1. Use Win32DiskImager to copy an image of the entire SD card to your computer's hard drive (`.iso` file).

2. Write the `.iso` file to a microSD card.

If the new RPi boots, you're in business. If it won't boot, here's how to copy data and programs over.

1. Put the SD card in the reader and list the files. You'll be able to copy files over just like it was a hard drive to a directory on the PC.

2. Replace the SD with a microSD already having an operating system installed. Copy from the computer to the microSD card.

Hard Drives

In this section, you'll learn about hooking up large standard hard drives to the Raspberry Pi. You may need a terabyte or three; it's possible, and a good entertainment system benefits from having such huge storage space available.

In the examples that follow, showing you how we add massive storage space for our entertainment systems by hanging hard drives from our Raspberry Pi boards, we'll be using Raspbian. How about something over *5TB?* That's a reasonably impressive start.

■ **Caution**   Large hard drives can easily draw more current than the Raspberry Pi can supply. As discussed in Chapter 2, use a powered USB hub rather than plugging drives in directly.

Connecting

Plug the drive(s) into the powered USB hub. In my case, I have three drives available: a 4TB, a 128GB, and a 1TB. Add those together and add the 32GB microSD card on this Raspberry Pi Model 3, and I now have 5,160 GB or 5.16 TB of storage space!

Now we need to find the drive's device name. We do that from a terminal (command line) window using the blkid Linux command (remember that Raspbian is a version of Linux optimized for the RPi). The command's name stands for "block identifier." Hard drives, in Linux, are block devices. So, running blkid, I get the information shown in Figure 3-5.

```
bin    dev   home   lost+found   mnt    mnt3   proc   run    srv   tmp   var
boot   etc   lib    media        mnt2   opt    root   sbin   sys   usr
pi@Mercer:/ $ sudo blkit
sudo: blkit: command not found
pi@Mercer:/ $ sudo blkit
sudo: blkit: command not found
pi@Mercer:/ $ ls
bin    dev   home   lost+found   mnt    mnt3   proc   run    srv   tmp   var
boot   etc   lib    media        mnt2   opt    root   sbin   sys   usr
pi@Mercer:/ $ blkid
/dev/mmcblk0p1: LABEL="RECOVERY" UUID="0403-0201" TYPE="vfat" PARTUUID="000f2819
-01"
/dev/mmcblk0p5: LABEL="SETTINGS" UUID="3c82293f-63d6-4338-a257-6808b7119fe2" TYP
E="ext4" PARTUUID="000f2819-05"
/dev/mmcblk0p6: SEC_TYPE="msdos" LABEL="boot" UUID="0501-9A24" TYPE="vfat" PARTU
UID="000f2819-06"
/dev/mmcblk0p7: LABEL="root" UUID="b58b874b-cab6-4573-b759-7919bfa740aa" TYPE="e
xt4" PARTUUID="000f2819-07"
/dev/sda1: LABEL="My Book" UUID="A2CA0AEBCA0ABC13" TYPE="ntfs"
/dev/sdb1: LABEL="1VID_1" UUID="3870C81A70C7DD2E" TYPE="ntfs" PARTUUID="5b6ac646
-01"
/dev/sdc2: LABEL="Toshiba" UUID="7070228A702256DE" TYPE="ntfs" PARTLABEL="Basic
data partition" PARTUUID="67761a10-d4af-4611-95d4-f67051fe2606"
pi@Mercer:/ $
```

Figure 3-5. *Finding attached hard drive devices*

"Mercer" is the name of this particular Raspberry Pi Model 3. I name all my computers and have for decades. Makes them easier to identify on the network and adds a bit of fun to things.

We're looking for device names identifying hard drives. I have three drives, so these three lines show what device names Raspbian has assigned them:

```
/dev/sda1: LABEL="My Book" UUID="A2CA0AEBCA0ABC13" TYPE="ntfs"
/dev/sdb1: LABEL="1VID_1" UUID="3870C81A70C7DD2E" TYPE="ntfs"
PARTUUID="5b6ac646-01"
/dev/sdc2: LABEL="Toshiba" UUID="7070228A702256DE" TYPE="ntfs"
```

That's good. I see enough information to tell me the first device is my 4TB drive, the second an old 128GB portable HD that was lying around here gathering dust, and lastly a 1TB Toshiba HD. Now that we know the RPi recognizes all three, we can configure them for use.

Configuring

Configure drives the right way and you'll have access to everything on them, like the complete run of "Buffy the Vampire Slayer" you're planning on binge watching. Luckily, making the disk usable simply means *mounting* it.

In the root directory (the topmost) in Raspbian (and indeed all versions of Linux) is the /mnt directory. Mounting a hard disk device there requires only one command. To demonstrate, let's mount my first device —/dev/sda1, the 4TB drive. We use two Linux commands, sudo and mount. The first gives us root (administrative) permission, and the second connects the device to the directory:

```
sudo mount /dev/sda1 /mnt
```

Good. It worked. I found this out by using the Linux ls command (list) on the /mnt directory. All the existing files are still there and now accessible on the Raspberry Pi.

But ... wait. I have three drives and only one mount directory? No problem. You can create directories of any name. Use an underscore character (_) instead of spaces in Linux.

For the purposes of this exercise, I (rather unimaginatively) used /mnt2 and /mnt3 for my other two mount directories. Thus, to mount them, I issued these two commands:

```
sudo mount /dev/sdb1 /mnt2
sudo mount /dev/sdc2 /mnt3
```

For this, we use the df -h Linux command (the command is short for "disk free," and the -h switch says to put the result in human-readable format). Figure 3-6 shows the result.

```
pi@Mercer:/ $ df -h
Filesystem      Size  Used Avail Use% Mounted on
/dev/root        28G  4.0G   23G  16% /
devtmpfs        459M     0  459M   0% /dev
tmpfs           463M  6.4M  457M   2% /run
tmpfs           463M     0  463M   0% /sys/fs/cgroup
tmpfs            93M     0   93M   0% /run/user/1000
/dev/sda1       3.7T  150G  3.5T   5% /mnt
/dev/sdb1       112G  173M  112G   1% /mnt2
/dev/sdc2       932G  839G   94G  90% /mnt3
```

Figure 3-6. *Seeing mounted drives*

The bottom three lines show the three hard drives mounted and ready for use. However, if you want them to be available every time the board boots up, a bit of quick editing is required. To make our connection(s) permanent, we must configure them into the `/etc/fstab` file. At boot time, Raspbian will check this file and connect the hard drive or drives in it.

To edit the file, you can use `nano`, which comes in Raspbian. Type:

```
sudo nano /etc/fstab
```

However, I prefer `emacs`. It's one of the first things I install on all of my Linux-based computers, and has been for decades. So a shout-out to this great, free, exceptionally powerful editor. Read about it here: `https://www.gnu.org/software/emacs/`. Install it on your RPi by typing:

```
sudo apt-get install emacs
```

Anyway, to make our hard drive connections permanent, we add our devices to the file as shown in Figure 3-7.

```
File Edit Options Buffers Tools Conf Help
proc            /proc           proc    defaults          0       0
/dev/mmcblk0p6  /boot           vfat    defaults          0       2
/dev/mmcblk0p7  /               ext4    defaults,noatime  0       1
/dev/sda1       /mnt            ntfs    defaults          0       0
/dev/sdb1       /mnt2           ntfs    defaults          0       0
/dev/sdc2       /mnt3           ntfs    defaults          0       0
# a swapfile is not a swap partition, no line here
#   use  dphys-swapfile swap[on|off]  for that
```

Figure 3-7. *Editing the fstab file*

By the way, the `ntfs` entry comes from running the `blkid` command and identifies the type of file system on the drive. Yours might be different, so enter that column appropriately so that Raspbian knows how to read the disk.

We leave the command line now and use a graphic terminal. In my case, TightVNC (http://www.tightvnc.com), a free remote-control software package). Figure 3-8 shows access to the drives. You now use them as you would files on any drive.

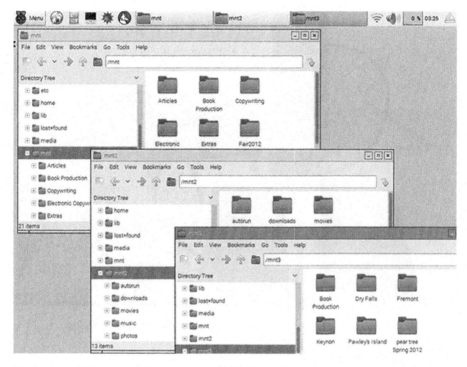

Figure 3-8. *All three hard drives now available for use!*

Should you discontinue using a drive, it's good practice to edit it out of the fstab file.

Figure 3-9 shows what all the hardware looks like, connected.

Figure 3-9. *My Raspberry Pi Model 3 with 5TB of drives and a powered USB hub*

What We Learned

In this chapter, we visited the two types of memory present on a Raspberry Pi. The first of those is working memory, also known as RAM (Random Access Memory). *Working memory* is *volatile*; it goes away whenever the board is powered down. *Storage memory*, like memory cards or attached devices such as hard drives, is permanent and allows us to retain programs, files, movies, photos, and so on.

We saw how to manipulate SD and microSD cards and to burn image files of entire operating systems and their file systems onto these cards.

Finally, we added vast amounts of storage by attaching hard drives.

Storage problems solved, we move on in Chapter 4 to an overview of available media center software.

CHAPTER 4

■ ■ ■

Constructing a Complete Media Center

We owe a lot to Thomas Edison—if it wasn't for him, we'd be watching television by candlelight.

—Milton Berle

The title of this chapter probably should be "Constructing and Using a Complete Media Center," but there's only so much room. That, however, would better cover the purpose of this chapter. We'll be looking at the building process, specifically getting everything ready for adding your media components.

As I write this chapter, classical guitar music streams off the Internet via Kodi (Figure 4-1) on a Raspberry Pi 3 to some Bose speakers. Background music, I've found, keeps me in concentration and churning out more words per writing session.

Figure 4-1. Using Kodi to play background music for writing

Let's dive in.

At this point, you'll want to have a means of input and output for configuration. A minimal setup should include:

- USB keyboard

- USB mouse

- USB or HDMI display

For the display—since we're building a media center—go ahead and hook it to the HDMI-enabled TV you'll be using. Just plug one end of an HDMI cable into the TV and the other into the Raspberry Pi.

It is assumed you know how to select the right input on the TV (that is, the one Kodi HDMI output from the Raspberry shows on your TVs screen) and that you can adjust the height and width of the picture slightly so that Kodi properly fills the screen, if needed.

Constructing a Basic Media Center

You've seen now how simple the installation of a bundle operating system optimized for Kodi is. Well, if you think it gets hard now—hooking a bunch of stuff up to the Raspberry Pi—no, it doesn't. Simplicity continues to rule, *as long* as we do a bit of planning ahead of time.

Hardware

By "hardware" here, I'm referring to items needed to connect an intelligent controller device into our media center.

Whoops. *Intelligent controller?* I'd better explain that term. It's a method of computerized automation. The Raspberry Pi is—you got it—a computer. The RPi, like larger computers, *multitasks*—that is, it runs hundreds of small programs called *processes* essentially simultaneously and also larger application programs the same way.

Think of it this way. It's as if instead of a credit-card sized computer you had 200 people standing around, each person excelling in a particular task. One might help you select a movie, and another would research the plot and actors in the movie. Yet another would lean in and show the movie's poster and other art work. And so on.

But you can't get that many people in your living room, nor afford to pay them to just stand around most of the day and night. So we use a $35 computer to emulate all those experts standing around until their one function is need.

That's an intelligent controller, a tiny computer running hundreds of processes each just waiting to do its little expert task.

It's the only way to fly.

Let's list the core necessities for an automated media center:

- A Raspberry Pi. We suggest the RPi 3 because it has the faster processor and comes with both WiFi and Bluetooth on the board. The latter two add convenience of placement as we'll discuss shortly.

- A nice-looking case for the Raspberry Pi. You want to protect it and show off the technical prowess at the same time. You do not want someone picking up a bare board and shorting it out with popcorn-greasy fingers. One you might like is the Flirc Pi 3, 2 and B+ case—it's made of aluminum and has a built-in heat sink (a piece of metal on the top of computer chips to help them dissipate heat better and avoid damage). Since an RPi used as a media center controller runs long hours, a heat sink to keep it cooler is a very good idea.

- A power supply for the RPi that plugs into the wall. This allows you flexibility in placement rather than having it plugged into a USB port on your computer. As stated in Chapter 2, you'll absolutely need one that provides at least 2.5 amps of current. You'll find that information in the small print on the unit plugging into a wall socket.

- Some sort of controlling device. A useful choice is a USB mouse and a USB keyboard for both point and click motions and text entry.

- A microSD card with 8GB or more (32GB is the max the Raspberry Pi can currently handle but is inexpensive, and I recommend you use one). Yes, even 32GB is much too small for a media center; but you saw in Chapter 3 how to get as much additional space as needed.

- [Optional] A powered USB hub. Absolutely necessary if you want to connect additional hard drives; USB CDs, DVDs, or Blu-ray players; remote control infrared receivers for remotes, and so on.

Those items represent the heart (or brain if you prefer) of your media center. We'll discuss other hardware needed in connecting various components as the need arises.

Figure 4-2 shows my Raspberry 3, the basis of my intelligently controlled home media center, in its protective case. Counter-clockwise from bottom left, the plugged-in cables and dongle are:

1. Power cable from a wall power supply

2. HDMI cable to TV

3. USB keyboard

4. USB wireless dongle for mouse

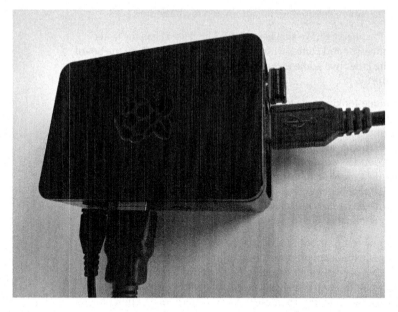

Figure 4-2. Raspberry Pi 3 configured and connected as a media center controller

Placement

The Raspberry Pi 3, keyboard, mouse, powered USB hub (if present) all should be on a table near the largest component, usually a flat-screen TV hanging on the wall. This is the primary control center and the place where new components get hooked into the system. Keeping it close to the TV means you don't have to run an HDMI cable all the way across the room.

Don't worry, we'll still going to have a remote control allowing us to flop down on the couch, binge-watch movies, eat popcorn, and quaff our favorite libation. See, I'm not losing sight of the true basics of home entertainment here.

Considerations for the table include:

- Positioning it near the TV, out of the way yet still readily accessible.

- A small chair so you can quickly and comfortably sit down whenever using the mouse and keyboard.

- Keep the cables and other wiring neat so that adding or removing components is easy and the backs of the units are accessible for plugging and unplugging. Trying to find the right cable in a rat's nest resembling the stereotypical "explosion in a spaghetti factory" wastes good viewing/listening time.

- An outlet strip attached to the top rear of the table is also handy to avoid having to get down on the floor in a darkened room to plug in a new device or remove an old one.

I've learned the hard way over the years the awkwardness of not being able to access the backs of units. So, I'm a big fan of a table with space behind it or at least one allowing ease of pulling it out a bit. Ease of access pays off over and over in pure convenience.

What We Learned

In this chapter, we did the basics of constructing a media center. We discussed the necessary hardware needed for controlling a home theater, along with the placement of your control center with ease of access for making changes.

In the next chapter, we'll be installing an operating system to run our Raspberry Pi and Kodi, the main application software that will deliver all that great entertainment for years to come.

CHAPTER 5

■ ■ ■

Let's Make a Media Center

The only people who have anything to fear from free software are those whose products are worth even less.

—David Emery

It's mostly free—that's the wonderful thing about the software for playing, recording, or otherwise manipulating media with a Raspberry Pi. We'll happily take advantage of that throughout this book, while giving shouts out to all the dedicated developers making this bounty of goodies possible. Thanks, wonderful programming folks.

Another thought is worth mentioning in this chapter's introduction. The first section—Chapters 1, 2, and 3, and 4—were rather general in nature. They were meant to give you a basic familiarity with the hardware and the various operating systems used to run the board. While you'll find this intro stuff useful many times, the reason you bought a ticket to ride through this book concerns, as the title states, learning the mastery of RPi intelligent media control.

The rest of the book is about just that, controlling, manipulating, and plain all out *enjoying* all sorts of media.

We start with something complex but easy to accomplish. We choose the right software, associated cables, and other hardware necessary for building a Raspberry Pi-controlled media center, one that fits your wants and needs or at least gives you the facilities to customize yourself into one soon enough. We then install the media center software and begin using it.

Kodi is the most popular media center software currently and is well supported (see `http://kodi.tv`). After reviewing the other options, I chose Kodi; however Kodi is much easier to install and use on the Raspberry Pi if we have a package consisting of an operating system optimized for the RPi and Kodi. More about that in a moment, but some general thoughts first about what a media center does for us.

What is a Media Center, Anyway?

A *media center*—sometimes called a *home theater*—consists of a computer-managed system for playing audio, showing video, displaying photos, and sometimes providing facilities for recording audio and video. Such systems also allow the management, storage, and retrieval of digital music, video, and other content, playing games, and much

© Ralph Roberts 2017
R. Roberts, *Mastering Media with the Raspberry Pi*,
https://doi.org/10.1007/978-1-4842-2728-2_5

more. Remote-control facilities, such as wireless or Bluetooth devices can be used also. All of this serves the usual purpose of these systems: home entertainment.

In Figure 5-1, one of my own tiny but powerful Raspberry Pi 3s configured with media center software runs an HDTV screen, streams movies from the Internet, plays music, and much more.

Figure 5-1. *The Raspberry Pi 3 has the memory and processing power needed for running your home theater*

Desirable functions of a media center include:

- Managing your video library

- Watching live TV

- Recording and creating a library of TV shows

- Finding and playing those shows (binge watch, even)

- Managing your music collection

- Playing music with high quality audio

- Delivering movies and video to HDMI devices like flat screen wall TVs

- Recording music and/or video

- Watching or listening to streaming Internet services (and there are tons these days)

- Remote control of your system via Bluetooth, network, even the Internet

- Playing DVDs and CDs

- Play video games

- And more

As to the last bullet point, editors sometimes do not like it when writers insert a vague statement such as "and more." In this case, it's meant to include flexibility, the future proofing of your home theater. New entertainment techniques, formats, and gadgets come along all the time. For example, a big trend now is automated speaker devices such as Apple's Alexa and Google Home. Tying and controlling these new things into your entertainment center as you acquire them is nice. So, the flexibility of "and more" should be an important feature to you.

Specifically, how do we add that flexibility? That's the basic underlying theme of this book—embedding an affordable intelligent controller in your media center. A controller with the processing power and upgrade capacity for adding and controlling all sorts of stuff we haven't even invented yet. The Raspberry Pi, of course, gives us that flexibility, covering many years to come.

The general term for all the preceding is *convergence* technology—more appropriately *media convergence*. That's the linking and control via computer software of separate technologies like playing movies and sound, finding digital content on hard disks or local networks, or even the Internet, and a host of other neat features we'll be looking at.

The key to all this very fine stuff depends on computers running the proper media center software. While the first personal computers, like the IBM PC, could do some of a home entertainment system's function back in the 1980s, the term "Home Theater PC" and the appearance of software devoted to controlling the entire system did not come about until the mid-1990s.

The personal computer did and still does quite a good job of managing and serving up music, movies, photos, and so on. However, even today, PCs remain expensive, too expensive to tie up running a home entertainment center when someone need to use them for word processing, balancing the checkbook, or one of the many other chores a PC does for us. So, the general trend now, in this day of SoCs, is to embed a small computer board dedicated to this one purpose—running your home theater.

Wow, that sounds like a great solution! What could we possibly use? Right, good suggestion (albeit something we already knew), a Raspberry Pi. At around $35 retail and with a huge base of free media center software, it's perfect for the job.

Let's look at some of these media software packages for the RPi. After that we'll chose one to build. As we go through the most popular systems, the obvious choice for simple yet powerful software will most likely jump out at you, but allow this little bit of suspense for the moment. Also, it's not inconceivable that one of the others covered here might be more attractive to you.

Popular Media Center Software

First, to have a powerful media center tailored to your tastes and requirements, there's no need for programming. The following software packages probably do most of what you want already and offer room for customization to add other features. Don't reinvent the wheel; just add some spinner hubcaps and other virtual customization.

Also, we're only looking at media center software here. Video and audio players, editing programs, various waveform manipulation such as DAC (Digital to Analog Conversion), and more are the topics of later chapters.

You'll also see here how to find, download, and install the media center software we're examining. Installing software, however, should not be confused with "building" a media center/home theater. That's just one step. To complete our center, we need to connect various components like TVs, sound systems, DVD/Blue Ray players, and so forth. We also need network devices to connect our entertainment center to the Internet, choose streaming services, and more.

For now, on to some of the top choices for a home entertainment controller, media center software running on a Raspberry Pi.

Here are the winners (envelope please).

LibreELEC

LibreELEC (http://LibreELEC.tv) is an operating system that includes Kodi (https://kodi.tv/), a popular entertainment center software package. Both LibreELEC and Kodi are open source (free for the download). LibreELEC is a *fork* of an older package, OpenELEC.

Figure 5-2 shows LibreELEC installed on a Raspberry Pi 3 booting up, but it also runs on earlier RPi models. I've been using it for months now, and this is the easiest way to go in building your own media center.

RELEASES MAY 26, 2017

LibreELEC (Krypton) v8.0.2 MR

LibreELEC (Krypton) v8.0.2 MR brings an update to Kodi v17.3, improved support for Intel WIFI and Bluetooth devices, performance enhancements to HEVC support on Raspberry Pi, and minor nip/tuck fixes for user-reported issues since v8.0.1. Kodi v17.3 addresses a notable subtitle (zip file) handling vulnerability that has been widely reported in the media. Changes since 8.0.1 include: Fix for zero byte AddonsXX.db files Fix for connman failing to enable ip_forwarding when using the hotspot feature Fix for minimum Audio Engine sample rate in Kodi (allows forced 48KHz) Fix for suspend issues with CX231xx DVB devices Fix for unreliable 1000-BaseT Ethernet on iMX6...

Figure 5-2. *LibreELEC's website supports this operating system + Kodi package, which installs and works nicely on the Raspberry Pi*

Kodi, by the way, is like the wheel we do not need to reinvent mentioned above. This feature-rich package runs under many operating systems and supports PCs, Macs, Linux, and other operating systems. In fact, I'm killing some of the suspense I also alluded to above, the complete media center we'll be building. Other choices in media center packaging also involve Kodi, as does the next media center package we'll be looking at in this one, OSMC. However, RasPlex (which follows OSMC) does not use Kodi. No one's saying you should use Kodi. You might feel RasPlex is the coolest of the cool. We'll see, but I love my Kodi center.

Features

In LibreELEC, we get a small, thus *fast*, operating system optimized for and including Kodi.

We, of course, are most interested in the Raspberry Pi builds.

Historically, home entertainment center software required large desktop computers. LibreELEC is designed specifically for *small form* computers, including single-board, System on a Chip devices like our beloved RPi.

43

Two significant shortfalls, until recently, have kept the Raspberry Pi from being all it could be as an embedded media center controller—memory and processing power. LibreELEC got around these detriments by employing a stripped-down version of Linux. Other operating systems for the RPi, such as Raspbian, have all sorts of services and other processes running in the background, multitasking and supporting the standard software which comes with the OS as well as all the programs you add. Entertainment center software, being very greedy for memory and CPU-time, bogs down small systems.

Yes, you can, for example, install Kodi on a Raspberry Pi running Raspbian or a good many of the other operating systems available for these boards. Slowness and hanging will be problems. No one wants a movie to stop for several seconds until the controlling board catches up.

For earlier models of the Raspberry Pi—the Model B, B+, and even the RPi2— LibreELEC was a great answer. It's an operating system with only services to support and run Kodi. It's so lean in fact that even with Kodi included, LibreELEC is only a tiny 561,192K (in size (that's the size of the image file after unzipping, just over .5GB). Contrast that to the image for Raspbian Jessie (latest version) which is 1.5 gigabytes or about 3 times larger.

The vastly lower consumption of limited on-board memory, processing time, and other resources speeds up Kodi and efficiently serves up movies, music, photographs, and whatever else you build your media center to do. Which is exactly what we want and expect. This efficiency makes choosing a $35 Raspberry a smart choice indeed and saves you perhaps hundreds of dollars that can be better spent on HDTV screens, speakers, DVD/Blue Ray players, and so on.

LibreELEC achieves even greater efficiency because it is written from scratch specifically for running entertainment center software on a Raspberry Pi, unlike most other solutions for that purpose. Other systems install on other versions of Linux— Ubuntu or Windows for desktop computers, or Raspbian for the RPi. Also, it's designed to make maintaining operating system software easy, meaning that all upgrades and additions can be done with the graphic interface. Keeping software up to date is a very good thing to do. You get bugs (glitches) fixed, improvements in operation as they come out, and new features. For this, you don't need to use any sort of management console, command line terminal or, indeed, know anything about Linux to use it.

Another advantage of LibreELEC is that it runs even better on the latest version of RPi, the Raspberry Pi 3. That gives you more memory and a faster, 4-core CPU team with LibreELEC to give Kodi a nice boost.

Install

Some might (okay, will) say, "Installing media center software's a pain."

No, it's not.

Oh, agreed, it was truly a pain setting up one of those old home theater TVs. Finding and installing the right drivers and getting Windows to run entertainment software is often enough more problematic then programmable. Windows can be and is balky sometimes or even worse; remember the Blue Screen of Death. I do, having seen it often enough.

LibreELEC greatly simplifies this process for us. Everything you need—operating system, drivers, and the Kodi entertainment center software—come in a quickly downloadable image file. Remember those? We met them in Chapter 3. Image files provide one of the Raspberry Pi's great advantages over bigger, far more expensive desktops. They let you change out operating systems in seconds. Yes, seconds. Just switch SD or more likely microSD cards these days, power up the board, and the new system boots. Want to go back to the previous operating system? Just switch the card. It cannot be emphasized enough how awesome and convenient and powerful this ability is.

I purchased an additional RPi 3 the other day with the intention of devoting it to controlling my media center fulltime. In about 10 minutes, I downloaded LibreELEC to my computer, unzipped the image, burned it to a 32MB microSD, and inserted it into the RPi. Booted up the RPi 3, which came up running Kodi. Did some minimal configuration, plugged an HDMI into the Raspberry Pi board, and was watching TV with my feet up.

Here, then, are the basic steps to install LibreELEC with Kodi on a Raspberry Pi.

1. Choose the right image for your RPi and download it at `https://libreelec.tv/downloads/`. To find the right file, scroll down the page until you see the Raspberry Pi berry trademark. Click the dropdown menu and click the top item, which works on both the RPi Model 2 and Model 3. Look down three paragraphs and a link in blue appears with the name of the image file—right-click on it so that you can specify your desired download directory. (Make this easy on yourself by downloading to a directory where you can find the image.)

2. The zipped file containing the image has a .gz extension. Extract it via 7-Zip (`http://www.7-zip.org/`) as discussed in Chapter 3.

3. Use Win32 Disk Imager (get it free at `https://sourceforge.net/projects/win32diskimager/`) to burn the LibreELEC image to a microSD chip (assuming you have a more recent board such as the RPi B+, 2, or 3). Using the maximum recommended SD card size for the Raspberry Pi, 32GB, is a good thing to do. You'll have extra room for enhancements to your system as needed. See Chapter 3 for a fuller explanation of burning images to SD cards.

You'll need to run Win32 Disk Imager as Administrator for it to have the right permissions to write the image file. Do this by right-clicking on the program's icon and, from the dropdown menu, left click on `Run as administrator`.

---

4. Wait for the image to finishing burning itself onto the microSD before removing it. The dialog box in Figure 5-3 shows when Win32 Disk Imager has completed its task.

Figure 5-3. This is how we know the microSD is ready for use

5. Insert the completed microSD into your RPi and apply power.

This process is quick and simple. There are only a couple of things you need to be careful with, and I'll show you those in a moment. Figure 5-4 is the first of a series of illustrations of this installation in progress.

Figure 5-4. LibreELEC's Welcome screen during its short install process

The entire process from inserting the SD card and applying power to the RPi to finish takes about three or four minutes. Very simple and your reward is Kodi, up and running, ready to entertain you for years to come.

The installation proceeds from the Welcome screen (which does some automatic configuration first) to the next one, in which Kodi assures us of its presence also (Figure 5-5).

Figure 5-5. *Kodi's coming on board!*

We will configure Kodi shortly.

Moving along, we now get a welcome screen (Figure 5-6), which informs you of a few very basic configurations for you to accomplish.

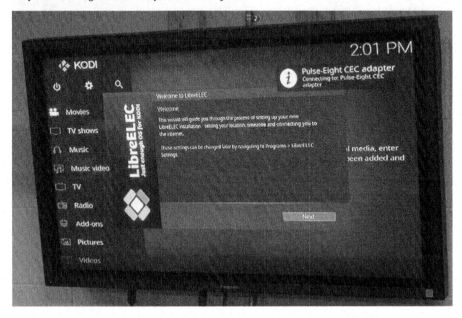

Figure 5-6. *The welcome dialog box appears, but you can see the main menu of Estuary (the default skin or theme of Kodi 17.3) already in place behind it*

Using your mouse, click the blue Next button and you are asked for an Internet connection with existing access points or wireless routers (Figure 5-7). If you have one of these, select the one you want to use. A connection is critical for downloading, streaming, and otherwise accessing the vast world of entertainment music, video, cat photos, and so on out there. If you do not have an access point, just run a network cable from your router or a network hub if you have one and plug that in the Raspberry Pi. This latter will need to be configured after we get Kodi running and is covered later.

Figure 5-7. *Selecting a connection to the Internet*

Click the blue button (Next) again and look at the next screen (Figure 5-8). It allows you to activate two services—SSH (Secure Shell) and Samba (used to connect with other computers on your local network). SSH allows logging in to the LibreELEC operating system for maintenance. You definitely need Samba (turn it on), and I highly recommend switching on SSH. You'll find it of use not only for maintenance but for things such as installing a few add-ons that can't be done within Kodi. And speaking of SSH, be sure to write down the default username and password shown in the dialog box.

Figure 5-8. *Turn on SSH and Samba*

Click on Next and you'll see Kodi's main screen, as shown in Figure 5-9. We're now ready to start using our media center. Yes, installation is a breeze, with just the few steps covered here.

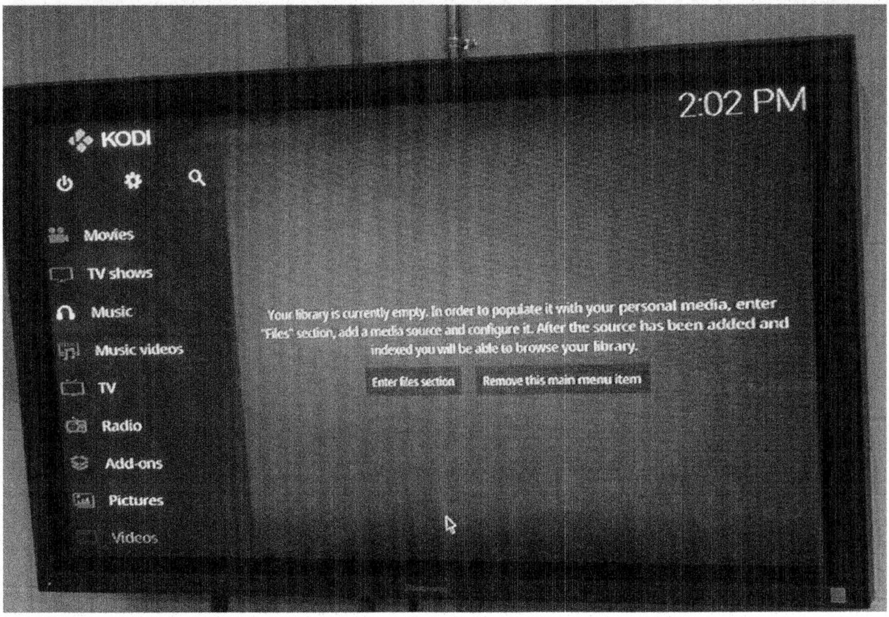

Figure 5-9. *Kodi's now ready to use!*

Kodi

That brings us to Kodi, an open source media center software package. Kodi is currently the most popular software solution for media control on PCs and especially small devices like the Raspberry Pi.

As described on its website (`https://kodi.tv`), Kodi, formerly known as XBMC, is an award-winning solution for or playing videos, music, pictures, games, and more. Kodi runs on Linux, OS X, Windows, iOS, and Android. It allows users to play and view most videos, music, podcasts, and other digital media files from local and network storage media and the internet.

You'll learn more about Kodi's features and operation in the next chapter.

LibreELEC bundles an optimized operating system and Kodi. It's also possible to install Kodi on a Raspberry Pi that already has an operating system. This, however, is not a good solution. When Kodi has access to fewer resources and must compete with many other processes for CPU time, it runs slower and even bogs down from time to time. Since the Raspberry Pi is so inexpensive, the better solution uses an optimized system.

Exploring Kodi

Those of you familiar with Kodi's previous version, 16.1, have already seen that it now looks different. Meet Kodi's new default skin, Estuary (Figure 5-10).

Figure 5-10. *Kodi 17.3's main screen comes up in the Estuary skin showing movies by default but getting to the other features is more direct than in the old theme, Confluence*

Gone is the Confluence skin, replaced by Estuary. This new theme provides a more direct path to Kodi's features, both the old and the new. I liked it from the first, but...

Returning to Confluence Now and Again

Yes, Estuary is the better skin for Kodi and easily mastered. However, should you wish to return to Confluence (again, for those of you who've used it)—I suggest only briefly, such as doing something you haven't quite mastered in Estuary yet. It's a matter of seconds to switch back and forth. Here's how:

1. Click on the settings icon at the top left of Estuary's main screen (the little gear symbol.

2. Click on Interface settings.

3. Move the cursor over the menu choice at the top, Skins.

4. Move left to the top bar in the larger portion of the window, which is labeled Skin and currently has Estuary on the right (as the current skin).

5. Click on the bar and a list of installed skins appears.

6. Confluence won't be there the first time you access this area, so click on Get more...

7. Scroll down the list of available skins and click on Confluence. It installs and you are up and running it.

In Figure 5-11 we see Confluence running on Kodi 17.3. It works just as you're used to. However, you should learn Estuary—it's truly better and faster than Confluence, a good step up in your entertainment center enjoyment.

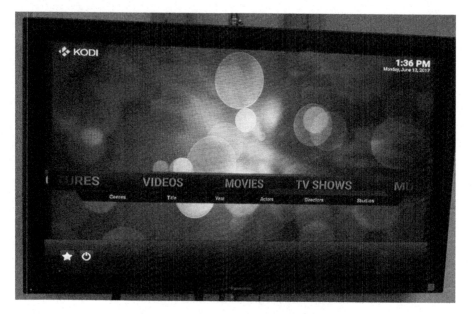

Figure 5-11. *The Confluence skin from Kodi 16.1 works fine on the new Kodi, but Estuary (the new default skin) gives fast access to features and configurations*

For returning from Confluence to Estuary, go to System / Settings / Interface / Skins. Click on the top bar and choose Estuary. Again, switching skins only takes seconds; and now that we've changed skins in both Estuary and Confluence, note that the procedure is the same. So, feel free to bounce back and forth as needed as you learn Estuary.

Now, let's get familiar with Estuary's main screen.

Estuary's Main Screen

While Kodi 17's operation remains the same under the hood (but with improvements and additional features) as previous versions, the default skin is cosmetically different. The major advantage is ease of operation. You don't have to go through as many levels as in Confluence to achieve results and, after all, we'll here to watch movies and listen to music. Complexity, we don't need.

We can also do without inconvenience. To me, a significant improvement is in navigation. Using Confluence, we have that horizontally scrolling bar on the main screen. Moving the cursor over the selections such as Video, Music, Pictures, and so on causes submenus to drop down. The *gotcha* in that concerns sliding the cursor down to the submenu you want. It's awfully easy, and frustrating, to touch one of the other major selections and wide up at a submenu of Video instead a Music one. Again, I'm here for the entertainment, no to improve my hand-to-eye coordination. (That's a lost cause.) Estuary makes it simpler to navigate.

So, here's a tour of the main screen.

To Your Upper Left

In the upper left of Estuary's main screen, under the Kodi logo, we find three small but important icons (Figure 5-12).

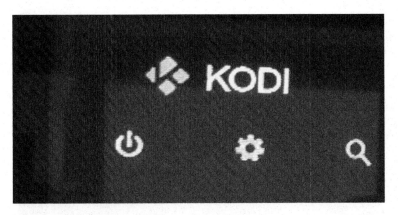

Figure 5-12. *Icons for power, settings, and search*

The leftmost icon is the widely used one for power on/off operations. Just like in Confluence, it offers three choices:

- Power off system
- Custom shutdown timer
- Reboot

The first turns off your Kodi / LibreELEC / Raspberry Pi system. The second allows you to program it to end in an hour or whatever length of time you select. The Reboot option causes Kodi to reset itself.

Settings More Convenient

In the middle of the three icons depicted above is a little gear icon often used, as it is here, to denote Settings. In this case, the configuration menus for Kodi and LibreELEC are gathered into one handy grouping instead of the several paths under the previous version. This grouping is a good example of the major difference in navigation convenience I spoke of earlier. We can now get to configuration submenus quicker.

Figure 5-13 shows the System screen of Kodi running the Estuary skin. Just click on the gear icon on Estuary's main screen and this one comes up, ready for configuration tasks. In the figure the Interface settings icon block is selected. This is the one we used in the example earlier of changing to the old Confluence skin.

Figure 5-13. *System screen that appears after you tap on the gear icon at the upper left of Estuary's main screen*

Search and You Shall Find

The final of our three icons on the upper left of the main screen is a small magnifying glass. Since that great detective, Mr. Sherlock Holmes, popularized it as a search tool, the magnifying glass has been a symbol of, well, searching. It is here also.

Clicking this icon activates a dialog box with four choices, as we find here:

- Search local library
- Search Add-ons
- Search YouTube
- Search the MovieDB

Click and fill in the fields to search.

Entertainment Please

Back to the main screen; Figure 5-14 shows it again for orientation purposes.

Figure 5-14. *Estuary's main screen with Movies selected*

All the menu selections below those three icons we've just finished exploring are for entertainment purposes only. Precisely the reason we're building our home theater / media center in the first place. At this point, I've made great progress and am enjoying my center (the one all these photograph show) immensely. It's a keeper!

When both OpenELEC and its fork, LibreELEC (my choice for Kodi 17.3) boot up, the Movies selection is enabled by default. So that's a good place to start in using our newly installed (or newly upgraded) media center software system.

Movies

As shown in Figure 5-14, Estuary boots up with Movies selected. The thumbnail posters are there and you're ready to choose and watch films.

As you'll see in Chapter 11 on importing movies, the Movies selection does not appear on Confluence's menu until we had movies in the library database. A significant difference between the Confluence and Estuary skins lies in the fact that all the possible categories—movies, TV shows, music, music videos, live TV, live radio, and so on—all show on the main menu from the first. If you have no library imports in that category, nothing shows except a message telling you that.

Again, referring to Figure 5-14 and assuming you have available movies, the main part of the screen shows three sections—the top part of the screen being sorting criteria (by year, genre, actor, and so on), the next movies in progress, and the bottom the most recently added. You can click on any of those to watch or resume watching from the farthest point reached in your previous session.

Clicking on the Movies main menu item, gives us the list of movies and associated data. As you run the cursor over a title, its plot, artwork, and so forth appear as we see in Figure 5-15. Note that this data appears if it was "scraped" off the Internet; again, see Chapter 11 for importing movies.

Figure 5-15. Information and artwork about each movie shows as you pass the cursor over the movie's title

Right-clicking a title gives us the editing and management choices for that movie. All these choices look and work the same.

Note the Options choice at the bottom left of the screen. Click on it and you'll get a menu with choices for changing the view, sorting, ordering, filtering, updating the library.

Oh, yeah. What about the procedure for importing movies?

1. Select Videos (toward the bottom of the main screen).

2. Click on Files.

3. Use Add Videos to set up a video resource directory.

4. Right-click on the resource directory now listed in the Files menu and hit Scan for new content.

TV Shows

The TV shows menu item comes next. As with Movies, we have category sorting icons on the top of the screen followed by TV shows in progress, and recently added episodes. You'll see how to add new series and episodes in Chapter 11.

Click on TV shows to see a list of series. Figure 5-16 shows the first screen after selection of TV shows.

Figure 5-16. *The TV shows menu selection makes it easy to browse and select from the shows in your library*

Music

Yes, the Music main menu selection operates in the same way as Movies and TV shows. See Chapter 10 for the procedures to add music resource directories and import into the music library. Figure 5-17 is Estuary's music screen.

Figure 5-17. *the Music menu selection follows the same pattern as Movies and TV shows*

Music Videos

Yes, I have no musical videos. Not yet. So, when I select Music Videos all that shows up is a message telling me that. However, in any empty section, we have two choices (see the two buttons under the message as shown in Figure 5-18 below).

The first choice sends us to Video / Files. We then follow the procedure you'll learn in Chapter 11. Adding a music video to the library is the same as adding a movie except, after creating a video resource directory somewhere on your network for music videos, take care during the scraping process to tag it as a music video so that Kodi knows which library database it goes in. Properly tagged, it shows up below instead of the empty library message shown in Figure 5-18.

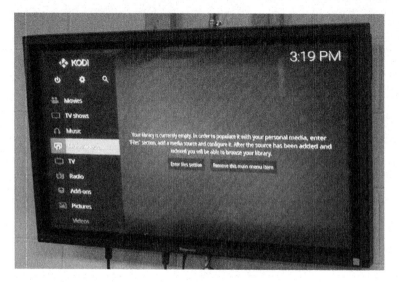

Figure 5-18. *This is what an empty library looks like*

The second choice removes this selection from the main menu. I choose to leave mine in place as, no doubt, I run across downloadable music videos and want a place to put and play them from.

TV

Yes, you can stream and watch live TV in the hundreds of channels using Kodi.

Radio

There are zillions of radio stations just waiting for your listening pleasure.

Add-ons

Add-ons, usually produced by third parties, give us a wide choice of features we can add to Kodi. We've already discussed add-ons in previous chapters but Chapter 15 ties it all together. A nice feature of the Estuary skin is that all add-ons are now available in one convenient place, that being the Add-ons selection on Estuary's main menu. Figure 5-19 shows how it looks when populated with add-ons.

Figure 5-19. *The Add-ons menu works the same as all the ones above, giving you access to and the ability to install third-party adds, enhancing Kodi with new features you select*

Pictures

Photos are media also and, as we'll see in Chapter 8, Kodi handles them well. Especially awesome, if you're into photography, is letting Kodi generate random slideshows of your photos. It makes a nice background to modestly show off your images to visitors without being obvious about it. "Oh, yeah, I took those," you say when they ask.

Figure 5-20. Kodi has powerful features for showing photographs

The Pictures selection is different from the ones for movies, music, music videos, and TV shows—there is no picture database. However, it gives you access to picture resources (directories you've designated as resources). These appear as icons when you click on this main menu item. Click on one of those, set up a slideshow, and you're good to good.

To start a slideshow, click Options and then View slideshow.

Videos

The Videos selection on Estuary's main menu gives you direct access to video resource directories as well as the Files icon where we can add more resources.

Favorites

Bookmark your favorites and access the links here. Figure 5-21 shows some of my bookmarks.

Figure 5-21. *Bookmark and access your favorites using the Favorites menu selection*

To bookmark any media, right-click its title and then click Add to favorites.

Weather

This selection shows the weather forecast for your area *if* you've programmed it in. To add weather forecasting is a two-step process. First, find a weather add-on that covers your area and configure it for the nearest large city. Second, in System / Service settings, configure your weather add-on to be the one Weather shows. More about the specific steps for this and how to get and install other add-ons in Chapter 15.

Kind of wish I hadn't added a weather service. Look at our forecast in Figure 5-22. Thunderstorms for the next five days! Ouch.

Figure 5-22. *Getting the latest weather info*

What We Learned

In this chapter. we first determined what a media center is and the desirable features it should have. We then chose a package containing an operating system optimized for Kodi, our media center software. That package, of course, is LibreELEC.

Next we downloaded the file from the LibreELEC system containing the image for the package. We unzipped that file and burned the image to an SD card. Inserting the card into a Raspberry Pi and applying power starts the install procedure. We found only two screens required input from us in this quick and pleasant installation.

Now, we start using Kodi.

CHAPTER 6

■ ■ ■

Optimizing Your Media Center

Entertainment is temporary happiness, but the real happiness is permanent entertainment.

—Amit Kalantri

Now that we've installed media center software on our Raspberry Pi, accomplished some configuration (more of that coming in this chapter and later ones as we need it) and, perhaps, attached some additional storage, we're ready to rock and roll. Quite literally, if you like that kind of music (I enjoy classic rock, for example).

In this chapter, we look at software, hardware, software, and then housekeeping. We begin by looking at software tweaks to make Kodi run faster in the Raspberry Pi's limited working memory. Several of the tricks coming up will speed up and smooth out your watching and listening enjoyment.

Software Fixes and Tweaks

We're concentrating here on changes easily made from inside Kodi using its menus. In more advanced chapters later, we'll visit the Linux command line for running software other than Kodi such as discrete video and audio players, manipulating waveforms, writing simple scripts, and all the other neat things the RPi can do.

Showing the Correct Time Zone

It's always nice to know the time showing on Kodi's screen is correct. On the Estuary default theme screens (the default theme Kodi comes up showing when first installed), the time appears in the upper-right corner.

When installed, not knowing which time zone you're in, that time will default to GMT (Greenwich Mean Time), now referred to as UCT or Universal Coordinated time, the locality being the Prime Meridian. Before someone catches me on it, GMT and UCT are slightly different (up to an interval of .9 seconds). The science of this is something beyond the scope of this book.

© Ralph Roberts 2017
R. Roberts, *Mastering Media with the Raspberry Pi*,
https://doi.org/10.1007/978-1-4842-2728-2_6

Anyway, in computers and many other fields, the GMT time zone has been where time zones start and end. That is, moving from east to west (the way the earth rotates in showing areas to the sun), we would go through 24 time zones (24 hours in the day) and wind up back at Greenwich.

Here in North Carolina, Eastern Standard Time is five hours behind GMT. So even though it was 7:20 PM when I finished installing Kodi for the first time, 12:20 AM showed on the screen, five hours ahead of my local time. Your time will vary depending on your time zone.

You probably prefer Kodi showing your local time.

The fix is simple.

From the Kodi main screen, select and click on System (the gear icon at the top left of the main screen), then Interface from the submenu which appears, and then Regional.

1. On the Regional menu, move the cursor down to Timezone country (do not click unless the country is wrong, otherwise click to change).

2. Move down one line to Timezone and click to change.

You now have a list of time zones on the screen. Choose the appropriate one for your locality and click. If you chose the right time zone, the time on the upper right of the TV screen will be correct. If not, pick a time zone that yields the right time.

Figure 6-1 shows the menu for picking your time zone.

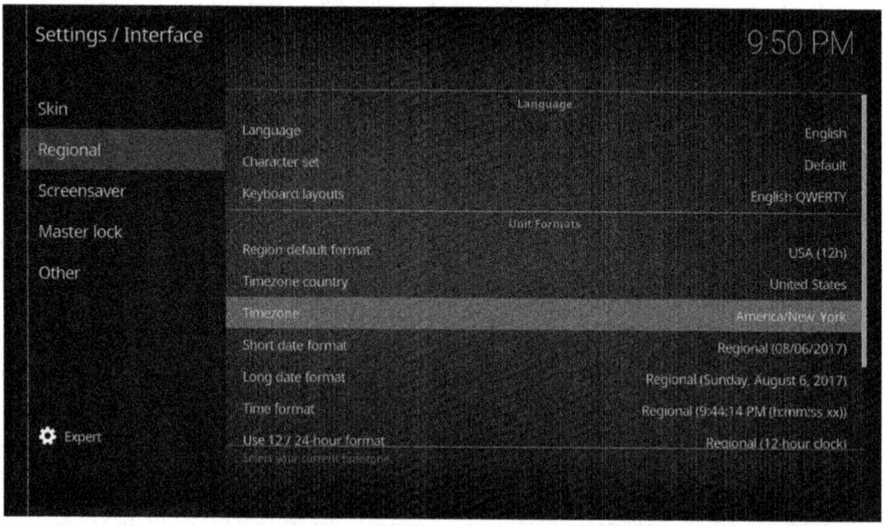

Figure 6-1. *Setting the correct time zone helps with scheduling and keeps your media center in synch in other ways*

By the way, don't worry about setting the minutes. Even if you change the time zone, Kodi keeps the correct minutes, which it gets from whatever time source the operating system consults on the net to keep the correct month, date, day, hour, minutes, and seconds. All we need to correct is the time zone.

Optimizing Kodi

Kodi, like any media entertainment software, performs resource-hogging operations in playing back video and/or audio. In fact, the best solution by far is devoting a computer solely as a media center controller. Of course, we've already determined these two obvious facts:

1. The Raspberry Pi 3, especially, is well-suited for media center control.

2. It's only $35 so, what the hey? Let's use it.

Number two above certainly makes the RPi the choice for so many of us. However, the very nature of a tiny, single-board computer—its lack of resources— can also be a drawback, but does not have to be. Limited memory, limited storage, and limited processing power all must be considered. Luckily, we can optimize (configure) Kodi to overcome these and give excellent results.

Did I mention the RPi is only $35 and LibreELEC/Kodi is free?

Yes, worth a little one-time effort.

Compare big computers to small, single-board ones.

The computer this book is being written on has two six-core CPUs running at 3GHz, 24GB of RAM (random access memory), about (counting on fingers) 9TB of hard drive storage. Darn right it'd make a fantastic you-know-what-kicking media center. Alas, it weighs over 40 pounds, is big, bulky, and would be a pain carrying from my office all the way home every day and hooking up to the wall TV just to watch a movie, listen to music, watch You Tube videos, and enjoy my other entertainment pursuits.

So, I now have an RPi 3 media center at home (like the one we've been putting together in this book). It's added fun and ease of use during the times of kicking back, shoes off, enjoying our home entertainment center.

Speaking of back, let's return to optimization of Kodi.

The specs of the RPi 3 include:

- Broadcom BCM2837 System on a Chip, which supplies a four-core CPU running at 1.2GH (Gigahertz).

- 1GB LPDDR2 (900MHz) working memory; note that the memory's slower than the CPU speed.

- microSD storage, 32GB recommended—and, yes, reading and writing to any SD card is usually significantly slower than to hard drives or the new solid-state drives (SSHDs).

Compare these resources to any desktop computer or laptop and you'll see there's a lot less overhead for running fancy embellishments, a good many of which Kodi has. That defines our strategy for optimizing Kodi—removing the unnecessary, thus increasing speed and smoothness of operation.

You can easily monitor your resources—memory and CPU usage—and see other information about your system in real time. Just go to System ➤ Systeminfo and you'll get the screen shown in Figure 6-2.

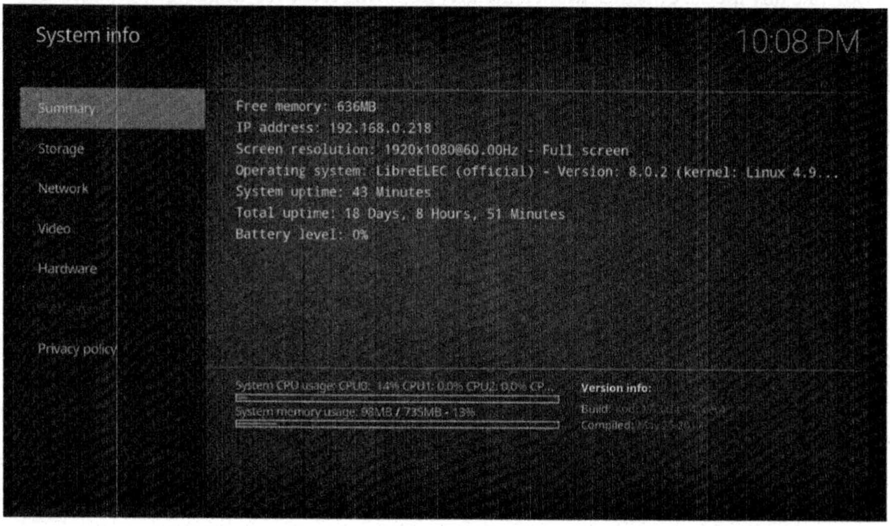

Figure 6-2. The system information screen. Check the various categories for more information.

We start optimizing with RSS (Really Simple Syndication), which is a means for delivering regularly changing information on a website to your local computer. Breaking news headlines is one, for example.

Stopping RSS

In Estuary—Kodi's default theme, the one it shows when first installed, and what you've been seeing in screen illustrations so far in this book—the RSS line at the bottom of the main screen (if RSS is enabled) scrolls information constantly. Although the information scrolled can be changed to news headlines or other items like most RSS feeds, the default (in LibreELEC/Kodi) provides us with blurbs about LibreELEC and Kodi.

The RSS items, again in the default configuration, includes announcements of new versions coming, the fact that LibreELEC won a certain award in 2014, Kodi has a new version arriving in 2017, on and on and on. After the first six million times, you might wonder if spending limited memory resources to stream this stuff is worth it. Let me save you around six million views. It's not.

So, it's recommended you turn off RSS.
To accomplish this in Kodi:

1. Go to System / Settings / Interface.

2. Move the cursor over Other (the color changes, indicating
    selection) and move the cursor on into the main portion of the
    screen.

3. Move the cursor down to Show RSS newsfeeds.

4. Click the oval with a dot in it to the right side of the line—if
    the dot is on the left, RSS feeds are off; on the right, they are
    enabled.

Figure 6-3 shows the screen you want.

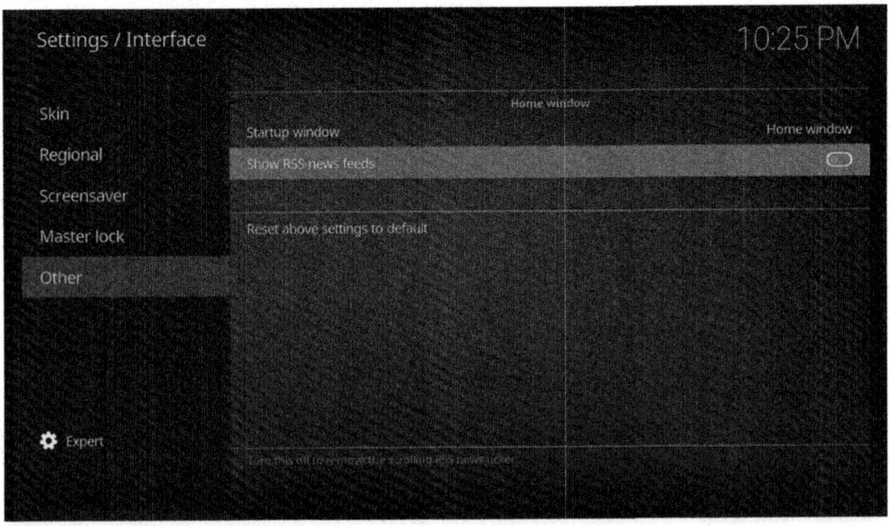

Figure 6-3. *Turn RSS off via this screen*

RSS is now disabled. You can always turn it back on if desired, but remember that it
costs resources and falls under the category of unneeded embellishments. Software bloat,
in other words.

To reiterate the point about the difference between desktops/laptops and single-
board computers like the RPi, there's a lot less headroom for unnecessary features. Paring
some of these away results in better use of resources. This means your entertainment
center streams movies more smoothly, and so on.

Turn Off Weather

Or, better yet, don't turn it on in the first place.

As the adage goes, everyone one complains about the weather but no one does anything about it. Kodi offers you several weather services as add-ons. You'll find these at System ➤ Settings ➤ Appearance ➤ Weather.

By default, in Estuary, the weather option is not enabled. To enable it, use the System ➤ Services ➤ Weather configuration menu to install an appropriate online weather service for your area. Again, access these system settings by first clicking the little gear-shaped icon at the top left of the main Kodi screen.

Weather sounds nice, but we don't have the extra memory and processor muscle to run it. Kodi would be regularly accessing the Internet, pulling down weather info. Better to look out the window.

Figure 6-4 shows the screen to get rid of weather; leave it set on None.

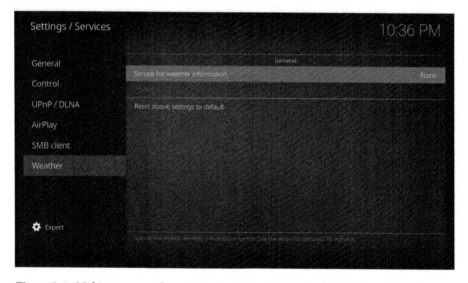

Figure 6-4. Making sure weather service disabled

However, if you decide that weather would be a nice feature, click the Service for weather information line, and Kodi presents you with a list of services to choose to select.

Resolution

Showing high-definition video screen resolution, such as 1080p (1920 × 1080 pixels) certainly takes more memory and processing power than the older standard of 720p (1280 x 720 pixels). When I originally wrote this chapter, I recommended setting screen resolution to 720p to give your Raspberry Pi media center a little more pep. However, after being dissatisfied with the picture quality, and running 1080p with no problems for

68

several weeks now, I say go for the best quality. Still, if you have problems, you can always switch back and forth easily, with these steps:

1. Go to System / System settings / Display.

2. Click on Resolution.

3. Select the resolution desired from the dialog box shown in Figure 6-5.

Figure 6-5. *Change the display resolution here*

Eliminate Unwanted Services

Underneath Kodi is LibreELEC (or whichever operating system you're using). LibreELEC in particular has been optimized to run Kodi but, like any Linux, still has numerous services running continuously, multitasking with all the things needed in controlling our media centers. Some of these services probably aren't needed for your purposes, so it's a good idea to free up more memory and processor time by turning them off.

In Kodi running on LibreELEC this is easily accomplished from within Kodi. Go to Systems ➤ LibreELEC ➤ Services. The configuration menu shown in Figure 6-6 appears.

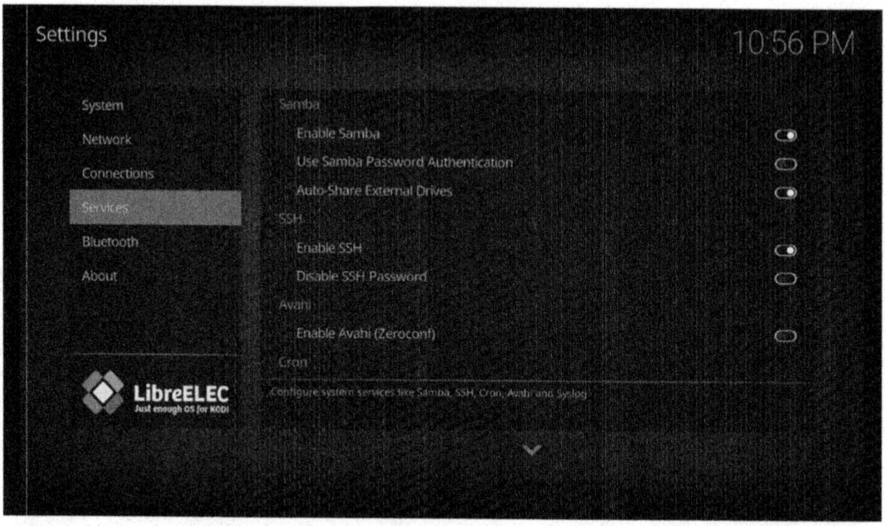

Figure 6-6. LibreELEC services settings menu

Let's examine each of these services and present you with some criteria for deciding if it needs to be running or not.

Samba

A collection of programs providing file and print sharing between networked computers, the Samba background service is activated by default in LibreELEC. This service makes copying files from computers on your network to external hard drive or microSD card storage on the Raspberry Pi possible. I recommend leaving it on.

Three settings affect Samba:

1. Enable Samba

2. Use Samba Password Authentication

3. Auto-share External Drives

Figure 6-7 shows how these choices look on the Samba configuration area.

Figure 6-7. Samba options

Click on any of these to turn it on or off. As we've seen before, in the default theme, the indicator circle at the far right shows blue for enabled and gray for disabled. Other themes use different colors.

The first choice, Enable Samba, closes the process or allows it to run in the underlying LibreELEC operating system. When the background processes making up this server are not running, we gain some processing speed and memory. However, as in life, background processes require compromises. Spending a bit of available resources on necessities is OK if you really need that service. Again, I think Samba is one such. Network access dramatically increases the power of your media center by allowing access to music, video, and picture resources on all your computers or other devices.

Choose Use Samba Password Authentication if the shared drives on other computers in your local network have password protection. In my own local network, all of which is behind a firewall, no passwords limit access to shared drives, so option 2 we leave disabled. Every bit saved is good.

If you have an external storage drive on your Raspberry Pi media center controller, sharing the drive is good (you be able to copy files over from other computers); make sure option 3 is enabled. The most important result is that you'll be able to copy videos, music, and other media files from shared drives anywhere on the local network.

SSH

Next down: SSH (Secure SHell) provides a trusted way of accessing the command line on a computer from another computer. To connect, the receiving computer must have an SSH server active—that is, it must be running the appropriate background process, as LibreELEC does by default.

The reason for doing this is to gain access to the RPi's operating system (in our example, LibreELEC) for upgrading, modifications, maintenance, and so forth. You may not want to have this capacity in a dedicated Kodi system but in our more advanced exercises later, you'll find it useful indeed.

To make an SSH connection from another computer, you'll need an SSH client on that computer. A good one (free) is PuTTY by Simon Tatham. Download it at http://www.chiark.greenend.org.uk/~sgtatham/putty/latest.html. You'll find versions for both Windows and Linux. Figure 6-8 shows what PuTTY looks like on my Windows workstation (I have lots of computers).

Figure 6-8. *PuTTY*

The default username and password for LibreELEC are:

```
root
LibreELEC
```

And here's what you see on the RPi running LibreELEC when logged in (Figure 6-9).

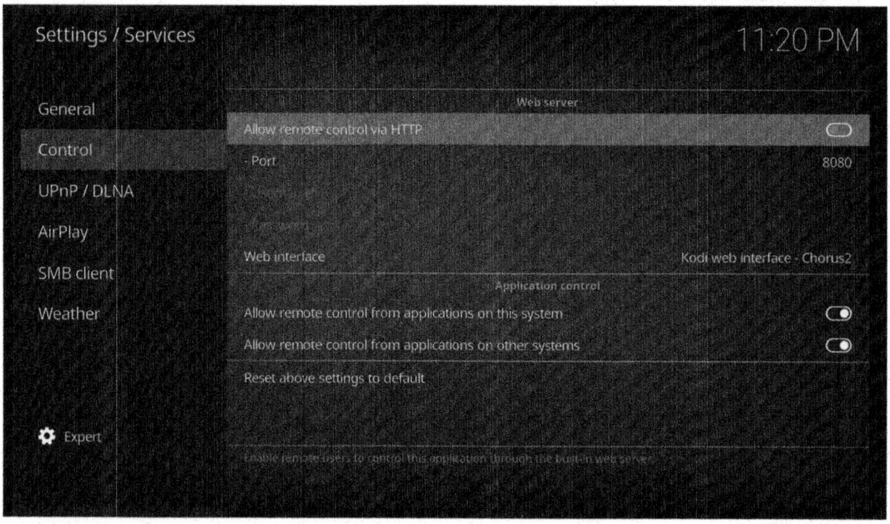

Figure 6-9. *Login screen seen after accessing LibreELEC via SSH, Sandy is the name of my RPi3 media center controller*

The two options for SSH configuration are

1. Enable SSH

2. Disable SSH password

My vote falls on the side of leaving SSH enabled. If you're sure you don't want to do command-line stuff, disable it to save resources. You can always turn it back on.

As to disabling password login, good practice says you want the protection of a password-required login. In other words, leave option 2 disabled always.

Avahi (Zeroconf)

Avahi is a type of zeroconf protocol, but there are others.

"Zero-configuration networking (zeroconf)," we can read in Wikipedia, "is a set of technologies that automatically creates a usable computer network ... It does not require manual operator intervention."

Well, as to that, on my local network we have something like 30 devices including smartphones, tablets, several Raspberry Pi boards, desktop computers, laptops, and a whole rack full of big-iron servers. With all those riches of possible connectivity available, Kodi only found the RPi it's on and two laser printers. Not too automatic, at all.

Meanwhile, Samba provides the connective services you and I need. Maybe other devices must have zeroconf installed and/or enabled but, for now, I recommend disabling zeroconf.

Cron

Cron is a time-based job-scheduling utility found in Linux/Unix operating systems. Kodi uses it for in periodically checking for updates, shutting the system down after a preset time, and it makes other scheduled events possible. If it's not on, enable it and leave on.

Drivers

This section current contains only the option to enable LCD drivers. If you do not have an LCD screen you want the Raspberry Pi that Kodi now lives on to run, leave this disabled.

Bluetooth

Bluetooth devices abound these days. Turn this service on to connect the Bluetooth-enabled devices below and more to your entertainment center:

- Computer mice and other pointing devices

- Keyboards

- Speakers

- Headphones

- Smartphones for remote control or file transfer

The two options initially visible in the Bluetooth section (see below) are

1.   Enable Bluetooth

2.   OBEX Enabled

If you have Bluetooth devices to connect, then enable this service. Otherwise, disable it and save resources.

OBEX is a service allowing file transfer over Bluetooth, such as to or from your smartphone. A good example of this might be downloading movies or music to your phone or pad for watching while on a trip. Enabling OBEX causes a third option to appear. It's used in designating which directory on the Raspberry Pi to store uploads in. The default is located on the microSD card. If you have an external hard drive hooked up, that would be the better choice.

Now, while we consider Bluetooth and in the neighborhood, look at the next choice below Services. Right, it's Bluetooth. Pass your cursor over it and to the right and we have the options used to connect (called pairing) Kodi with Bluetooth devices.

Wipe Out the Web Server

As you saw earlier, it's possible to use a browser on your laptop, pad, and so on to remotely control Kodi though its built-in web server. We also determined this was not a very good way of control. In our quest for to save resources, the web server is a great candidate go away. Here's how:

1.   Go to System / Services / Control

2.   Click on the top line, Allow remote control via HTTP, and make sure its disabled (the little indicator turns gray)

And the screen looks as shown in Figure 6-9.

What We Learned

The main concept we mastered in this chapter is the importance of optimizing our Raspberry Pi entertainment controller. Realizing that Kodi was originally developed for devices with a lot more memory and processing speed than single-board computers possess, we compromise by disabling unnecessary features, preventing them from bogging down our RPi. The RPi 3 then runs our media centers smoothly and efficiently.

Now, we move on to the features and operation of Kodi on a Raspberry Pi.

CHAPTER 7

Kodi in General

Americans don't spend billions for entertainment. They spend it in search of entertainment.

—Unknown

Now that we've installed media center software on our Raspberry Pi and optimized it for smooth operation on a single-board computer, let's find out what it does. This chapter shows you:

1. Hardware tips about hooking things up to our RPi media center controller.

2. Software in a more comprehensive look at Kodi's features and operation.

First, we hook stuff up.

Choosing and Attaching Components

A media center controller needs a media center to control. Some of these entrainment-providing devices you already have. A TV, for example, is the biggest and most likely central focus of the media center, so to speak. We'll start there and connect it first.

TV

First, a few words about TVs in general.

As far as media centers go, your TV is the elephant in the room. It's big, obvious, and shows colorful moving pictures with sound. In showing off what your media center can do, you'll no doubt immediately use the TV and show your guests some of the Kodi-driven features. To top off the "gosh-wow" stuff, point out the tiny case of your Raspberry Pi controller. Remark knowledgeably about how this tiny computer turns your media center into a powerful, smart home theater—because it does.

© Ralph Roberts 2017
R. Roberts, *Mastering Media with the Raspberry Pi*,
https://doi.org/10.1007/978-1-4842-2728-2_7

TVs today are wonderful; most likely yours is a large, thin, flat device hanging on the wall. Flat-panel technology drastically changed displays of all types. No more bulky CRTs (Cathode Ray Tubes) for computer displays or televisions. Flat-panel displays also made laptops, smartphones, and all sort of other electronic goodies possible. Flat-panels exploded into use because of their thinness, low power requirements, and downright convenience.

These screens fall into three basic types:

1. **Plasma**: Shown in Figure 7-1, a PDP or Plasma Display Panel was once common in large flat-screen TVs. They were invented in the earlier 60s, but manufacturing costs did not come down to make consumer televisions affordable until about 2004. The name "plasma" derives from the method of creating images, which involves using many small cells having electrically charged ionized gases (called "plasma").

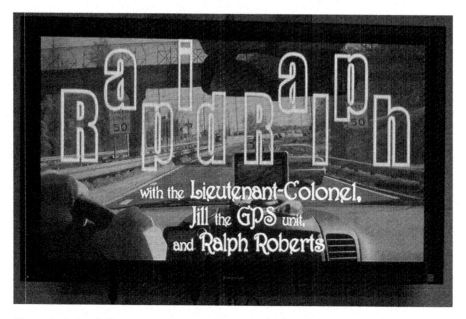

Figure 7-1. A 42" Plasma screen on the wall of my office used for video production (opening credits from a surprisingly popular local TV show I did for several years). Plasma's color reproduction was superior for years until OLED came along.

2. **LED**: The name *LED (Light Emitting Diode)* for flat-screen displays is a bit misleading. Most screens labeled LED really use LCD (Liquid Crystal Diode; a diode is a two-pole semiconductor allowing current flow in one direction). LCDs suffer from low light emission, so some form of backlighting is needed for bringing out the brightness and color we expect from our TVs. This backlighting was originally provided by fluorescent and still is in cheap units. LEDs became the backlighting solution, giving not only sharper pictures and more accurate colors than fluorescent lighting but presenting the added benefit of being more energy-efficient.

3. **OLED**: the third and newest type is OLED (Organic Light Emitting Diode). OLED displays do not use LCDs for generating the image. Instead every pixel in this type of display consists of a material that glows when electricity is applied. It's been described in an article by tech writer Geoffrey Morrison on http://cnet.com as "... kind of like the heating elements in a toaster but with less heat and better resolution." The organic part comes from the organic compounds enabling the various screen colors.

Assuming you don't have a TV yet, which is best?

For many years, plasma won hands down. It had darker blacks and sharper colors than LCD/fluorescent and the current LCD/LEDs. In 2006, flush with a big royalty check, we laid out $3200 for a 42″ Samsung plasma TV. Today, for about a tenth of that price, you can score an even larger LED screen that certainly approaches plasma's picture quality. Plasma TVs remain expensive and are disappearing from the consumer market. Two giants in TV manufacturing, LG and Samsung, discontinued their plasma models in 2016, for example.

Today, the choice would be LCD/LED, hands down on both price and availability. These units sell for low prices, and the picture quality gets better every year. LCD/LED remains a compromise but one we can afford. Table 7-1 sums up the differences.

Table 7-1. *Differences between Plasma and LED TVs*

Display	Screens	Viewing Angle	Contrast	Motion	Color	Power
Plasma	42″ - 65	Excellent	Excellent	Excellent	Excellent	Good
LED	19″ - 94″ Very Good	Very Good	Good to Excellent	Excellent		

Tomorrow, your choice will become better as the cost of OLED goes down. OLED screens, as of this writing, remain priced out of reach for most of us. However, this is truly cool technology, surpassing plasma. While plasma has great blacks compared to LEDs, OLED achieves absolute blacks and exceptionally bright whites down to the single pixel level! Currently, LG makes all OLED TVs, although other companies are working on them. Their picture quality is fabulous in its clarity, color reproduction, and viewing (some OLEDs screens curve for better, more realistic viewing).

Let's get back to hooking up whatever TV you have. I'm hanging on to my beloved plasma for the moment, but larger screens at economical pricing certainly tempt.

HDMI Hookup

The first media center connection we make to our Raspberry Pi/LibreELEC/Kodi controller is the TV. As suggested previously, place the RPi close to the TV, allowing you to use shorter cables, for one advantage.

Make sure your HDMI (High Definition Multimedia Interface) cable has the right plugs on each end. The Raspberry Pi comes with a female HDMI connector, as do TVs. So, we need a standard male-to-male connector, as shown in Figure 7-2.

Figure 7-2. The HDMI cable you need has ends as shown here

Mechanically hooking the RPi media center controller to the TV is simple:

1. To protect the circuitry, remove power from both the Raspberry Pi and the TV.

2. Plug one end of the HDMI cable into the RPi and the other into the TV.

3. Restore power to both.

4. Use your TV's remote to rotate through the inputs until you see Kodi's main screen.

Congratulations, you now have a computer-controlled media center. Well, at least they're connected and, just like this, you can use Kodi for all sorts for things. However, for great entertainment, we need Kodi to have greater control of not only the TV but its current and future peripherals also. After all, this is the prime reason for building a media center controller—to get the fullest control possible.

Next, you'll see how that's done.

CEC

CEC (Consumer Electronics Control) is built-in to HDMI and permits users (that's us) to control up to fifteen devices. The huge advantage of using CEC for our media center is two-way communications through the HDMI cable, which lets us use our existing remote to also control Kodi.

Full control requires two-way communication. Let's revisit the best way of enabling the TV, and whatever's attached, to provide data back to Kodi. Such control includes (as listed in the Kodi Wiki (http://kodi.wiki/view/CEC; lots more info about CEC there):

- Controlling Kodi from the TV's remote control

- Automatically switching to the right TV input device

- Letting Kodi control what mode your audio receiver is on when the TV switches on

- Turning all devices off with one remote

- Setting volume/mute of the receiver

Using CEC, you can also customize buttons on your existing remote. This allows flexibility in adding Kodi-controlled functions to the remote.

Turning on CEC in Kodi

The Raspberry Pi GPU has CEC support, which is thus available to Kodi. To turn on CEC in Kodi and configure it, go to System ➤ Settings ➤ System ➤ Input ➤ Peripherals ➤ CEC adapter.

You start with the Settings icon in the upper-left of the main screen (the gear symbol). Figure 7-3 shows what the CEC configuration screen looks like.

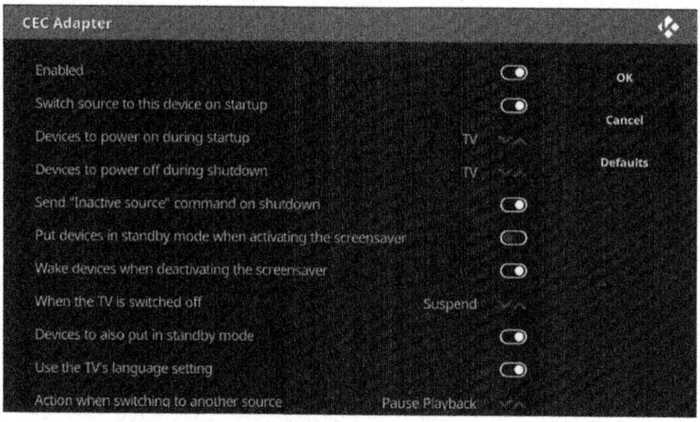

Figure 7-3. *CEC configuration screen in Kodi*

You also need to enable CEC on your TV. The option to do so is in its menus. Check first using the remote to search for it; otherwise look at the manual or just Google the model of your set and search for "enable HDMI-CEC."

Determining if Your TV Supports CEC

The good news is that almost all manufacturers include CEC in their sets today, but it gets a bit complicated. Yes, they have CEC; they just don't call it that! Again from http://kodi.wiki/view/CEC, following is a list of major manufacturers and how they label CEC:

- AOC: E-link

- Hitachi: HDMI-CEC

- LG: SimpLink

- Loewe: Digital Link or Digital Link Plus

- Mitsubishi: NetCommand for HDMI

- Onkyo: RIHD (Remote Interactive over HDMI)

- Panasonic: VIERA Link or HDAVI Control or EZ-Sync

- Philips: EasyLink

- Pioneer: Kuro Link

- Runco International: RuncoLink

- Samsung: Anynet+

- Sharp: Aquos Link

- Sony: BRAVIA Link or BRAVIA Sync (You may need to use a port labeled HDMI-MHL if the regular HDMI port does not work).

- Toshiba: Regza Link or CE-Link

On the web site, there are lists of specific models known to work with Kodi via CEC control, information about programming CEC functions, and more.

It's more than worth a little effort to add CEC control to your media center. Also, if you can control Blu-ray players, video recorders, and other peripherals through HDMI/CEC, you have a truly powerful and flexible media system that can grow as you add things to it.

What If There's No CEC on the TV?

If your TV was made a decade or more ago (like the one in my home), it might not have CEC. In such case, use the older infrared remotes. You won't have nearly the power as with CEC but it still makes operating your media center more enjoyable. In my case, I've got my eye on a 65" screen for under $500, and that fixes *that* problem.

Game Controllers

Got a game controller? No problem; Kodi has you covered there as well. Go to System ➤ Settings ➤ System ➤ Input ➤ Configure attached controllers. Figure 7-4 shows what that screen looks like.

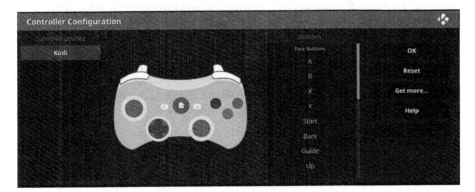

Figure 7-4. *Kodi lets you configure and use a game controller*

Sound Outputs and Inputs

OK, your TV comes with, again most likely, speakers built-in. Perhaps you've also added a sound bar and/or surround speakers, going for the whole theater effect, all connected directly to the TV. That's good and, assuming you have a CEC-enabled device and have activated CEC on Kodi's System ➤ Settings ➤ System ➤ Input Devices ➤ Peripherals ➤ CEC adapter menu, you're good to go. So, why would you want to input music or other sound coming into the RPi or output to sound devices (speakers, headphones, and so on.) directly to the Raspberry Pi? These connections, of course, may be either physically plugging in a cable or wireless.

Some major reasons include these:

- Driving speakers in other rooms via Bluetooth or WiFi
- Feeding Bluetooth headphones
- Streaming video/audio to mobile devices (covered in next chapter, including Netflix, Hulu, and so on)
- Connecting high-end audio DAC (Digital-to-Analog Converter) devices to get better sound

That's just a few, but all four of these uses can dramatically improve the utility of your RPi-controlled media center.

Take remote speakers. They've become quite popular of late, reproducing digital music with exceptional quality with wide range and deep pounding bass. I have several, but my favorite is a Bose Mini II SoundLink. With my Kodi software, taking the speaker anywhere in my house or office or sitting outside under a tree using my laptop is easy. We can use our smartphones as remote control of our media centers. Changing music streams is a breeze so long as you're in range of your system.

In later chapters, we cover not only adding sound systems to Kodi systems but also using the Raspberry Pi to acquire and stream music and video without using media center software. All sorts of possibilities and, right, the RPi is so cheap we can use them as embedded controllers in all sorts of projects, sound-related and more.

Let's review ways of sending sound from the Raspberry Pi to transducers. A *transducer* is a device which converts an audio signal into soundwaves the human ear can hear. Speakers and earphones are good examples of output. A microphone—a type of transducer converting real-world sounds into audio signals—is a type of input device.

Methods of outputting audio signals via the Raspberry Pi are

- HDMI socket for high-definition input and output of audio and video as well as control signals and other data via the CEC protocol
- The 3.5mm audio/video socket
- USB receptacles
- GPIO pins

HDMI: Having just connected an HDMI cable between our Raspberry Pi and the TV, I know it's necessary. But what if you have two or more HDMI devices—such as Amazon Firestick or Google Chromecast—and want to control them as well? Search online for "HDMI switch." You'll find many of them—including two, three, four, and five cable versions—in the $10 to $30 range. An easy problem to solve, but do read the reviews. Some seem prone to problems with automatic switching between cables, but in general such switches allow lots of scope for expanding your RPi-controlled media center.

Audio Socket: The 3.5mm audio/video socket is a standard like the headphone socket on smartphones and all sorts of other devices. Like smart phones, the one on the Raspberry Pi is also a 4-pole socket. On the phone, you have left channel audio and right channel audio (stereo), a microphone input, and a ground. The RPi socket is different in that it outputs video instead of receiving audio from a microphone. You can still use a microphone and input voice or live music, but the methods of doing this most often involve the USB receptacles, four of them on the RPi 2 and 3.

The RPi's socket is cleverly designed so that, despite having video output, it also accepts a standard three-pole mini-plug such as those on headphones and provides stereo sound. Just plug in your headphones. Very neat, see Figure 7-5 for the location of this jack.

Figure 7-5. *A Raspberry Pi 3 with the 3.5mm jack at the edge of the board center. To the left is the HDMI jack, and on the right edge are four USB receptacles with a cable plugged into one.*

USB: Basically buying one of the plentiful $5 USB soundcard dongles provides microphone and other audio input as well as better quality stereo sound output.

Additionally, many other sound/music related USB devices can be hung off our little single-board computer powerhouse. These include (again using Amazon as example for pricing):

- USB sound adapter ("dongle," from $5 up), adds soundcard to RPi.

- USB 6 channel external sound card 5.1 surround sound, about $14.

- 7.1 USB external sound card audio adapter.

- Creative Sound Blaster Omni Surround 5.1 USB Sound Card with High Performance Headphone Amp and Integrated Beam Forming Microphone, about $80 (use powered USB hub for this one).

- ELEGIANT USB Powered Sound Bar (also USB hub for power), $30.

- Focusrite Scarlett 2i2 (1st GENERATION) USB Recording Audio Interface, about $100.

- 5-Channel Battery Powered Mixer Professional Compact Audio DJ Mixer Controller with USB Interface, a little over $50.

That is just a random sampling. With USB, you have thousands of other choices from simple to just as high-end professional as you want. There is lots of flexibility and capacity to add all sorts of stuff to your media center.

GPIO: One feature setting the Raspberry Pi apart from much larger computers are the GPIO (General Purpose Input/Output) pins. These 40 pins allow the RPi to control a multitude of real world devices from doorbells to huge electric motors. More to our purpose in building media centers, they also provide a way to plug additional boards into the Raspberry Pi, called *tophats*. These boards have sockets matching the 40 GPIO pins and just slide into place.

This is not an advertisement, but I own two tophat boards made by HiFiBerry, the DAC+ - Pro and the Amp+. The difference between these two is that the DAC+ requires an amplifier while the Amp+ has a 25 watt per channel amp (with separate power supply) on the board that plugs into my Raspberry Pi, as shown in Figure 7-6.

Figure 7-6. *HiFiBerry Amp+ 25 watt per channel stereo amplifier tophat board plugged into Raspberry Pi. Note that you don't lose the use of your GPIO pins for other connections; they're passed through the Amp+ board.*

These boards both have audiophile-level DACs, markedly better than using the one on the RPi board or even a USB-connected DAC. When paired with good headphones or speakers, the HiFiBerrys give wondrously clear and deep basses and excellent hear-every-instrument-in-the-orchestra clarity. This may or may not be for you but it makes a good example of what's possible with your Raspberry Pi in the realm of great sound. These boards work with your RPi/LibreELEC/Kodi media center. Kodi recognizes the boards (once installed properly) and gives you control of whichever you have installed.

A little about me. Back in the day I owned and ran two stereo stores, specializing in top-of-the-line audio equipment. I was certified by the Society of Audio Consultants and came to truly appreciate good sound. The fact that I can get even better sound from a $50 add-on board (or $60 for the Amp+) than came from the old-technology analog equipment costing many thousands of dollars that I sold back then truly awes me. I revel in listening to quality digital records or even my collection of direct-to-disc records.

How good is good?

Both boards use a dedicated 192kHz/24-bit high-quality Burr-Brown DAC. This technology provides truly high end sound quality. The beauty of it is that both boards just plug into the RPi. They're not kits, no soldering, no cables required. Plug, configure, listen.

We'll look at high end-audio in more detail in later chapters, but let's get back to Kodi and how to use it.

Kodi Features

First, where did Kodi come from? According to information on the official Kodi website (http://kodi.tv), the original software was created in 2003 by a group of like-minded programmers. Team Kodi consists of unpaid volunteers from around the world. More than 450 software developers, the site tells us, have contributed to Kodi to date, and 100-plus translators have translated Kodi into over 65 languages.

A Brief History

The parent organization, the XBMC Foundation, was formed in 2009 to deal with mounting development costs, paperwork, and travel costs to developers' conferences and tradeshows, and so on. The XBMC Foundation is a nonprofit organization with the mission of developing great software.

The XBMC name derives from Kodi's first incarnation back in 2003. It was created as independent third party media center software running on the popular game console, Xbox. Not surprisingly, name of this software was Xbox Media Center, known by its acronym of XBMC. XBMC was a hit, and soon versions were coded for Android, Linux, BSD, macOS, iOS, and Microsoft Windows.

Wait for it, things are coming together here. A standalone Linux version (based on Ubuntu, called a "fork") came out under the name Kodibuntu. In August, 2014, the XBMC Foundation decided new versions of XBMC would henceforth be known as Kodi and registered the name as a trademark.

The Purpose of Kodi

As to Kodi itself, here's how the official description of Kodi (from `http://kodi.tv/about`) begins: "Kodi® (formerly known as XBMC™) is an award-winning free and open source (GPL) software media center for playing videos, music, pictures, games, and more. ..."

It's worth noting here that Kodi is "open source" under the GPL or GNU General Public Library license. That means any of us can get the source code for the program, modify it however we like, and distribute our own version. Warning: Should you do this, come up with your own name for the package—the name Kodi is protected by trademark.

More realistically, those programmers among us might want to write their own add-ons or, another type of plugin, skins. It's allowed. Kodi has a common API (Application Program Interface) allowing the creation of binary add-ons with C/C++ or script add-ons via Python scripts. That's deeper than most of us want to go, but lots of programmers out there—thanks to Kodi's popularity—are doing it and distributing some quite useful ones. Later in this chapter, we'll look at those.

The site continues, informing us that Kodi runs on Linux, OS X, Windows, iOS, and Android. Users can play and view most videos, music, podcasts, and other digital media files from local and network storage media and the internet.

They conclude with how easy it is to get help, saying "our forums and Wiki are bursting with knowledge and help for the new user right up to the application developer. We also have helpful Facebook, Google+, Twitter and YouTube pages."

Kodi is indeed the preeminent media center software; hence the decision to spotlight it here. To recap its advantages for us Raspberry Pi users:

- It's free!

- Kodi is comprehensive software covering most functions of a media center, and it's easy to customize and/or add additional features on demand.

- It runs on the Raspberry Pi, enabling a "$35 solution," giving you a dedicated computer that automates and controls your home theater.

- Once you become familiar with its features, menus, and operation, Kodi's a breeze to use.

Which brings us to what the rest of the chapter covers—the major features of Kodi.

Kodi Main Features

This section introduces you to Kodi's general features. Actual operation comes in the next section, where we'll explore all the screens making up Kodi's GUI (Graphical User Interface).

Keep in mind that Kodi—through skins and add-ons as two examples—allows many ways to customize and enhance this entertainment center software. The Kodi Team continues developing new versions, and there's also a lot of third-party support thanks, as noted earlier, to Kodi being both open source and popular. For now, in this subsection, we explore the major features of Kodi. In other words, answering the question of "what does it do?"

In general, Kodi supports the most widely used audio, video, and image formats, playlists, audio visualizations, slideshows, weather forecasts reporting, and third-party plugins. It is network-capable (Internet and local networks). The following sections look more specifically at these areas.

Music

Kodi plays pretty much any digital format used for music you throw at it. It has cue sheets, tagging, MusicBrainz integration, and adds smart playlists for almost total control of your music collection.

Audio formats supported by Kodi include these:

- MIDI

- AIFF

- WAV/WAVE

- AIFF

- MP2

- MP3

- AAC

- DTS

- ALAC

- AMR

- FLAC

- RealAudio

- WMA

- And others

By "and others," I mean "a lot." The Kodi Wiki refers to support for "a countless number of formats and codecs."

Playing Music

Playing music is accomplished from Kodi's main screen (Figure 7-7) or the full screen visualization. We'll do that shortly.

Figure 7-7. *Like many writers, I find backgound music helps me concentrate and stay at the keyboard longer. Calm Radio is one of the thousands of add-ons for Kodi and presents hundreds of hours of, as the name implies, calming music. All free.*

Music Library

In addition to playing music—selecting a digital music file from local storage, a computer on your home network, or on the Internet and listening to it—Kodi's Music Library offers functions with wide-ranging features. The wiki listed earlier offers many pages of information on how the library works. Following are some of the library's major features:

> **Adding music**: Kodi scans music files, searching for identifying data. If the music is "tagged," Kodi records this tagging information (such as artist, album, year, genre, and so on) and stores it in a database, allowing you to search by artist or any of the other tags. Yes, we turned this off earlier while making Kodi run more efficiently in the limited space of a Raspberry Pi; turn it back if you'll willing to sacrifice performance for this sort of completeness.

> **Music navigation**: The library sorts your music into categories and offers several methods of finding a specific file or files, and lets you sort and/or add filters to further narrow searches.

> **Music tagging**: Good music tagging is a necessity to use the library features to their fullest. The Kodi Wiki covers tagging in detail.

Cue sheets: When putting together playlists for CDs and other external media, the cue sheets feature gives you a standardized way of passing readable index, playlist, performer, songwriter, title, and so forth.

Music videos: Kodi can include music videos in its Music Library. All scanned music videos (that show in their tags as such) are listed in both music and video playlists. You can search various sources and download music videos using add-ons called "scrapers."

MusicBrainz metadata: MusicBrainz is an Internet database (https://musicbrainz.org) serving as an open music encyclopedia that collects music metadata and makes it available to the public. Kodi can query MusicBrainz for tag information on your untagged music.

Ripping CDs: The library provides several functions that allow you to build and burn music CDs; these are explained in detail in the Kodi Wiki.

Movies and Other Media

Another area Kodi emphasizes on the official site is viewing movies. The software supports all the popular video formats and sources, not the least of which includes streaming online media—movies on demand, for example. Kodi, if you have tags active, imports these movies with full posters, fan art, disc-art, actor information, trailers, video extras, and more.

I'll show you how to obtain and watch movies in the next chapter, but this is a good place to discuss Video Library functions. As it does with the Music Library, Kodi contains a host of features for cataloging and managing movies, TV, videos, and indeed media of many types (Figure 7-8).

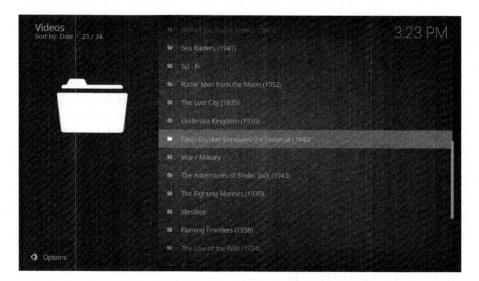

Figure 7-8. *I enjoy the old B and serial films of the classic era, so the Classic Cinema add-on was a no-brainer for me. Had to have it.*

Let's look at these in general. Being familiar with the concepts will help you when we start using and enjoying Kodi.

Media Sources

One of the true advantages of enjoying a smart, Internet-connected media center is all the media you can get practically instantaneously. Movies, cat videos, songs, photos, and so on and so on. Kodi makes searching for and downloading this plentiful bounty of great stuff. Whatever you might be in the mood for, chances are you can find it.

What makes this magic possible in Kodi are *Media Sources*. Media Sources are virtual links you set up, showing Kodi where to find, retrieve, and play such media as:

- Those on storage attached to your Raspberry Pi media controller

- Computers on your local network

- Sites on the Internet allowing media file downloads

Setting up Media Sources in Kodi requires minimal effort, and the software gives you helpful assists in doing so. To get a head start on your own, got to System ➤ File Manager ➤ Add Source and follow the prompts. You can have essentially as many of these links as you like, adding or deleting sources at any time.

In the next chapters, we'll do several examples in the different media file categories so you'll be up to speed on using this powerful feature. When you first start with Kodi you should at least add one source, like a drive or directory on your Kodi device to get you started. Copy some media files into it and you're good to go. Earlier in this book, we've already seen how to connect to other computers and hook up external drives (Chapter 3).

More powerful links can be activated in Kodi through add-ons. For a quick overview, if you select one of these three menu choices on Kodi's main screen—Pictures, Music, or Videos—the small dropdown menu shows two choices, Files and Add-ons. Hundreds of add-ons exist, allowing you to add almost any online media source you could ever want. Even commercial ones like NetFlix, Amazon, and Hulu. You still have to pay for such premium services, however.

TV Shows

Back in a not-so-long-ago day, we used to think that Direct TV and Dish were hot stuff— wow, a hundred or even two hundred channels. Well, using Kodi's Media Sources feature you can have literally *thousands* of channels on any given night. Beyond cool, eh?

With all the content out there, we need help, and Kodi gives us a TV show library (part of the overall movie and video library). The TV shows library (as described in http:// kodi.wiki) "supports episode and season views with posters or banners, watched tags, show descriptions and actors. Video nodes/tags and smart playlists can further organize your library for special interests, making specific screens for sci-fi, anime, etc."

PVR and Live TV

Kodi also provides features for showing live TV, including video recording (DVR/PVR). Kodi has an integral PVR (Personal Video Recording), which can connect to one of the many "backend" TV servers that are available. There are also lots of add-ons providing content, See Chapter 16 for more information.

This incredible wealth of content makes Kodi a true joy. Kodi's open source software encourages third-party programmers to constantly create new add-ons, bringing us even more content. That's good, very good indeed, but it also might get us in trouble if we're not careful.

Streaming video onto our TV via Kodi or in any other manner is OK so long as we have the right to do it. If it's in the public domain, free is cool. If it's copyrighted material through a for-pay service like Netflix, Hulu, and so on, we need to have a paid subscription and the right to stream it.

I'm mentioning this because there are a good many add-ons, some rather popular, that allow the watching of paid TV without the minor detail of paying for the content. No, I'm not listing them and you won't find them in all the add-ons listed in Kodi for download and install. So, just fair warning. Should you get one of those legally questionable add-ons, you could be setting yourself up for trouble. Remember all the suits over music downloading. This is the same thing. Not worth the risk since there's so much legal stuff out there.

Pictures

Kodi helps you catalog and manage all your photographs as well. I shoot photos all the time, sometimes several hundred a month. Kodi lets us import pictures into a library, scroll through them, set up slideshows, filter them and more—all using just our remote control.

UPnP

Here's another nice feature. UPnP (Universal Plug and Play) permits devices on the same network to see each other and connect. Kodi employs UPnP to stream to and from Kodi software running on other computers. Remember, Kodi is free—you can have it on your desktop, laptop, everyone in the family's phone, and stream shows or movies or pictures from and to your media center.

Add all the features to what we've met in preceding chapters, and Kodi's desirability as our media center software becomes increasingly obvious. And because it's free and the computer to run it, our Raspberry Pi, is so inexpensive, the possibilities just keep growing.

What We Learned

We looked at the differences between modern flat-screen TVs, starting connecting things by running an HDMI cable between our Raspberry Pi and the TV. We discussed CEC remotes, which allow two-way communications between HDMI devices—meaning that the RPi controller can give commands and get feedback from the devices it controls. We learned about the different methods of hooking speakers, headphones, and so on. to the Raspberry Pi—HDMI, 3.5mm audio jack, USB, and through the GPIO pins using plug-in "tophat" boards. Then we went over some of Kodi's major features.

Coming up next, we do a deep dive into Kodi's menus and start really using those features.

CHAPTER 8

■ ■ ■

Pictures and Video

The Internet? Is that thing still around?

—Homer Simpson

Now comes the time to begin the mastering of Kodi—for entertainment purposes only, of course.

I have a simple process of learning new software and new things in general and sincerely believe it'll work for you as well. May I suggest, as we explore Kodi, you follow along. Having a keyboard and mouse attached to your Raspberry Pi, as I described in Chapter 5, allows you easier navigation and the ability to type in commands and configurations. Highly recommended.

In this chapter we'll try out Kodi's functions, using the default Estuary skin, by setting up two kinds of resources, Pictures and Videos. Gentlemen and ladies, start your screens.

Pictures

Use a mouse or the arrow keys on a keyboard and move the cursor over PICTURES on Kodi's main menu (on the left side). The selection turns blue to show it's now selected. Do not click yet; let's discuss what we see when the cursor just hovers over the category selection. The majority of the screen (right) now shows the Pictures category as in Figure 8-1.

© Ralph Roberts 2017
R. Roberts, *Mastering Media with the Raspberry Pi*,
https://doi.org/10.1007/978-1-4842-2728-2_8

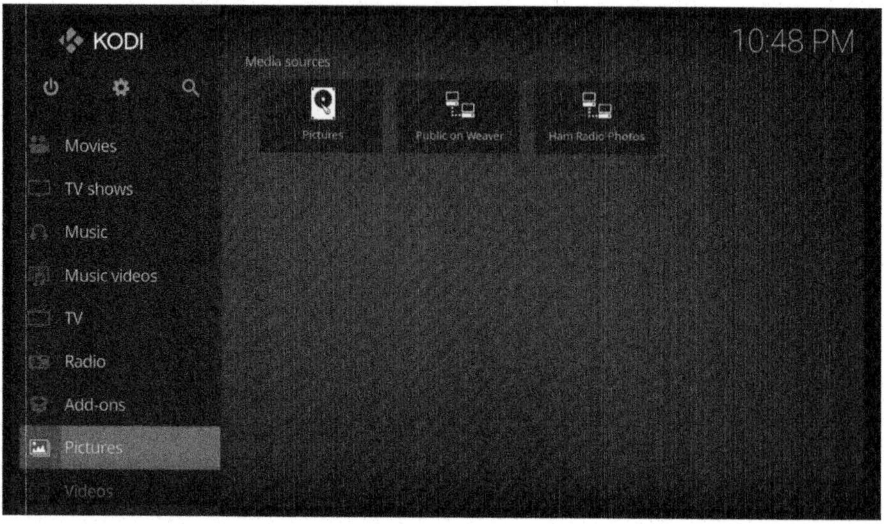

Figure 8-1. *Selecting the Pictures option on Kodi's main menu*

As shown, I've already added two links to picture resources residing on another network computer—Public on Weaver and Ham Radio Photos (my favorite hobby, so I take lots of photographs). Later in this chapter, we'll be setting up your own picture resources. Clicking on the ham radio link gives access to thumbnails of my pics (Figure 8-2). Clicking on any one of them brings it up full screen. Or I can do automated slide shows with each picture or other illustration showing in sequence.

Figure 8-2. *One of my photo resources; that's me in the center and my callsign, W5VE, on the antenna enclosure fence*

Picture resources of friends, family, hobbies, trips, events, and so on are fun. Kodi provides powerful ways of tracking and presenting our photographs either for our own enjoyment or to entertain visitors.

Now, back to your cursor hovering over Pictures on the main menu. Click now. The screen changes to the list in Figure 8-3. Again, I have resources already, but the point of interest for you here is the bottommost menu item, Add pictures. That's how we find and add picture resources.

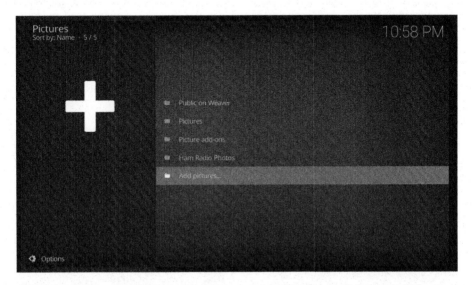

Figure 8-3. *Add Pictures lets us add picture resources to Kodi, creating virtual photo albums and slide shows*

Keep these three screens in mind; we'll be coming back to them shortly. However, this is a good place to add more information on how to navigate around Kodi.

Navigation

As we explore, here's a couple of tips on how to navigate back up from all the submenus we'll be visiting.

> **ESC key**: if you have a keyboard attached (recommended for ease of entering text), press the ESC key and Kodi returns you to the main menu (home screen).

> **Right-click the mouse**: Clicking the right mouse button is a fast way of moving back up through the menus.

> **Arrow icons**: Some menus have a left-pointing arrow icon; clicking on it also takes you back up a level.

External Drives

Pictures, music, and videos all require lots of storage space. I recommend a 32GB microSD card for the Raspberry Pi. That's nothing compared to the space any good media center will need. So, consider adding external drives and networked resources.

External drives are those hooked directly to your Raspberry Pi, the easiest to add (see Chapter 3) being USB drives. To repeat the warning about attaching devices requiring high current such as external drives, use a powered USB hub. The RPi on its own does not have the power capacity to run big drives, but it can certainly read and write to them for your benefit.

One immediate difference is the first item in Figure 8-3, the My_Book item. In Chapter 3 we saw how to add additional storage to our media center. Specifically, I added a 4TB (four terabytes; that's a lot) drive—a My Book from Western Digital, hence the name. Left-click on the name of your drive or drives (those physically attached to the Raspberry PI), and you'll get a directory listing as shown in Figure 8-4.

Figure 8-4. *External storage drive listing*

You could, once more, using powered USB hubs, attach several large hard drives to your Raspberry Pi and they would show up on the Pictures screen. This gives you tons of room for storing pictures, music, movies, video, and so on.

By the way, when we get to the Video and Music selections on the main menu, you'll see that these hard drives also appear there as well. Kodi, like most powerful software, offers several paths for getting to storage and other resources.

Internal Storage

Right-click your mouse to come back up one level to the `Pictures` menu. In Figure 8-3, we see an item also named `Pictures`. It links you to the `Pictures` directory on the internal storage device inserted into your Raspberry Pi.

In my case, internal storage is a 32GB microSD card. Storing media on the microSD card is a bad idea, *a very bad idea*. It suffers from slower retrieval and can quickly eat up free space better dedicated to the operating system, LibreELEC, and Kodi itself. If, for example, you only have an 8GB card, about two HD (high definition) movies and your system locks up, because all the room for swap files and working memory is gone.

That said, yes you can use it for photos or other media you want quick access to. Currently, I only have one photo in this directory, as shown in Figure 8-5.

Figure 8-5. *The Pictures directory on the RPi's internal microSD storage*

When a photo in any directory is selected, Kodi shows you a list of info about it. And, just a reminder about navigation, clicking on the arrow icon takes you back up a level.

To show a photo from the list in your Pictures directory on the internal storage, just click on it with your mouse or remote. It then pops up on the screen. The photo in Figure 8-6 is an example of my science fiction "art." I'm a rocket kind of guy.

Figure 8-6. *Clicking on the photo thumbnail shows the image full size on the screen*

A couple of things you can do while the photo's displayed. With the mouse, left-click on the photo, and Kodi adds animation to it like photos in documentaries. This is random. The photo may move slowly toward you or from one side to the other, and so on. This makes displayed photos more interesting while you talk about them to visitors.

Right-clicking with the mouse or hitting the Esc key on the keyboard takes the picture off the screen and returns you to the directory listing. If your mouse has a scroll wheel, scroll down to move to the next picture in the folder, or scroll up to move to the preceding picture. There are equivalent keys on remotes as well. Which one depends on how you've programmed it, but total control of the screen is always possible.

Back to the Pictures directory listing (which works like all directory listings). The top line of the dialog box sports an upward pointing arrow and two dots. Click on it and you go up one level, which takes us back to the Pictures menu as shown in Figure 8-3.

Picture Add-ons

To begin this topic, click Add-ons on Kodi's main menu and you will get the Add-ons screen shown in Figure 8-7. Four of the selections in this menu—those concerning video, music, programs, and pictures—include the capacity for add-ons (free mini programs that add features to Kodi). As you move the cursor over each menu item, installed add-ons for that category are shown.

I have a few add-ons already installed in this sample media center (see Figure 8-7). Like almost all resource add-ons, these require an Internet connection to work. The last two items (My add-ons and Download) allow us to configure or remove installed add-ons. The last, Download, facilitates finding, downloading, and installing desired enhancements to Kodi.

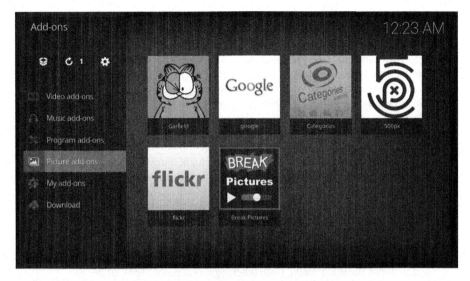

Figure 8-7. *The Pictures ➤ Add-ons submenu shows installed add-ons*

At this point, sliding the cursor over and clicking an add-on icon causes it to run.

We've moved the cursor down and are hovering over Picture add-ons as shown. Click on that selection and the Add-ons ➤ Picture add-ons screen (Figure 8-8) comes up.

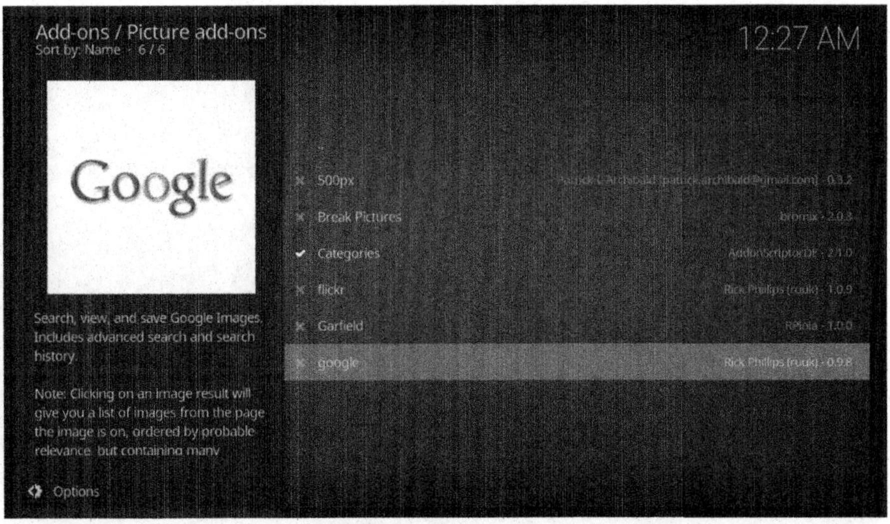

Figure 8-8. *The Pictures ➤ Add-ons submenu shows installed add-ons*

An add-on for searching and retrieving media from Google Images is highlighted. This gives access to millions of photos and other graphics on Google. We'll use it as an example of how to find and install add-ons in general and picture adds-ons specifically.

Before we continue, many more sources of add-ons exist than the ones we can find and install through the default Kodi software. Just Google "Kodi add-ons." However, it must be said, be careful downloading add-ons from other sources. Even those through Kodi are of varying quality and some may not even work.

Why?

As we've discussed before, Kodi is open source, meaning that anyone can write third-party add-ons for Kodi without getting permission or going through any sort of vetting process. It's good and bad. Good because a lot of hardworking folks turn out great add-ons. Bad because quality control and respect for legalities (as in copyright issues) are lacking in some add-ons.

I've uninstalled the Google Images add-on so we can restore it again together. (To delete an add-on, go to My add-ons, click on the category such as Pictures, right-click on the add-on, and click on Information ➤ Uninstall.) Here's the procedure to find and install a picture-related add-on:

1. From the main menu, go to (clicking on each one) Add-ons ➤ Downloads ➤ Pictures.

2. Scroll down the list to view and select add-ons for installation.

In Figure 8-9, I've scrolled down and highlighted the Google Images add-on. By the way, if there's a check mark next to the add-on's title, this means it's already installed in your Kodi.

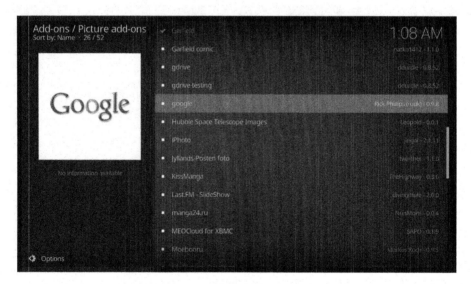

Figure 8-9. *Looking at available picture add-ons*

Let's install it as an example of how add-ons are installed.
Click on the title for the one to be installed. You get a screen like Figure 8-10.

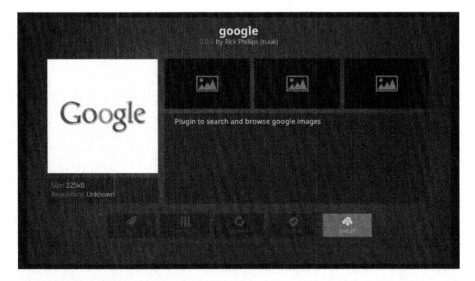

Figure 8-10. Add-on information dialog box

Click on Install and Kodi downloads and enables the add-on. During this
process, Kodi sends you back to the list of available picture add-ons. When installation
is complete, a check mark appears beside the title, and the add-on is ready to use. Go to
Add-ons ➤ Pictures and you'll see the new add-on's icon. Click it and you're ready to go.

Now, before we get too far from Figure 8-10, you can return to this information
screen for a specific add-on by simply right-clicking the title or icon for that add-on
anywhere you find it, and then clicking on Information in the drop-down menu that
appears. For an active add-on, an Uninstall icon appears where the Install icon
appeared earlier. This is how you remove an add-on.

In general, the other icons, moving left from the Uninstall one (at least for this
add-on), allow disabling or enabling, doing a manual update (better to have automatic
updating turned on), various configuration, and the little rocket lets you run the add-on
from that there.

▓ **Note**   By saying "in general" I mean that third-party add-ons come (in their thousands)
from programmers outside of Kodi. You'll find many variations in them, but (generally) the
information screen lets you do whatever needs doing for that add-on.

101

Oh, and what does the Google Images add-on do? Figure 8-11 shows an example. I searched for "Switzerland" and it returned lots of photos. Click on one to view or to start a slideshow.

Figure 8-11. *Google Images add-on*

Add Picture Sources

To add picture sources—directories on the Raspberry Pi SD or attached hard drives, or on your local network, or on the Internet—we want to create a permanent link. Begin by clicking Pictures on Kodi's main menu, and then on the bottom choice on the resulting menu, Add Pictures. In the dialog box that pops up, click Browse. The menu now appearing allows creation of links to sources of pictures on other computers, either on your local net or the Internet. The menu in Figure 8-12 is the one we're looking for.

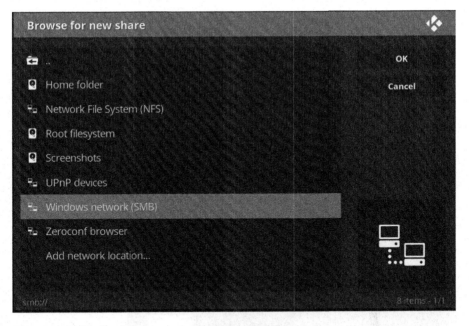

Figure 8-12. Browse for new sources of pictures and link them

We have several methods of connecting to sources on other computers:

Home folder: Connects to the home folder on the Raspberry Pi's microSD card. While using this location as a picture (or video) source is fine on a larger computer, it's a bad idea to take up the limited space on the microSD card with media files. Don't use it.

Network File System (NFS): a method of sharing files found (more often) on Linux systems. An NFS server should have nfs:// as the first part of its link address.

Root filesystem: The root system of the underlying Linux operating system on your Raspberry Pi. Don't mess with it unless you know what you're doing. Certainly, never try storing media there.

Screenshots: A folder for storing screenshots. The default has it in the home folder on the microSD card. Later in this chapter, you'll see how to change it to a better location, such as on an external or network drive.

UPnP devices: A set of protocols enabling networked devices to discover each other and communicate over a network. Chapter 16 shows using these to stream live TV among other things.

Windows Network (SMB): SMB (Server Message Block protocol) allows sharing network resources, such as connecting to other computers over the network. This is an easy way to link to directories on your desktop or laptop computers. Click on each computer to see drives shared on the network and to navigate to subdirectories. Figure 8-13 is an example of using Kodi to see and connect to the computers on my network.

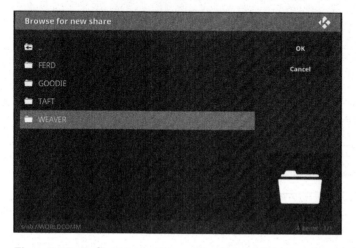

Figure 8-13. Kodi sees computers on the network;click to navigate to the directory you want. (This depends on permissions being set properly for network access)

Zeroconf Browser: Zeroconf (aka Bonjour) is another set of network protocols. If you browse under this option and have devices on the network with this protocol, this menu option lets you see and connect to them or a resource directory (that is, one with pictures) on them in the same manner as SMB.

Add Network location: Works the same as Windows Network (SMB) earlier.

Here's how to do an actual link, using linking to a directory on a Windows computer as example.

1. Click on a network protocol or location on the list in Figure 8-11.

2. Choose a computer or other device on your network or elsewhere and navigate to the directory desired or an Internet location.

3. Click the OK button on the right and the Browse for new share menu goes away, leaving the Add Pictures source dialog box—click on the Add button, then OK, and you're finished.

I've chosen the directory with my ham radio pictures mentioned earlier and named it Ham Radio Photos.

Once you've selected a directory or other location and set it up with the dialog box you get by selecting the link, return to Kodi's main menu and click Pictures again. Look at the Pictures menu (Figure 8-14) and we find my new link inserted (the one under my external drive link). From now on, just click on that link and it opens the Ham Radio Photos directory on the linked computer. This is a fast and convenient way to access media without having to store it on your Raspberry Pi. Click Add Photos again to create additional photo sources.

Figure 8-14. *The Public line above links to the Public directory on one of my networked computers and serves as a picture source; any picture in that directory and its subdirectories is viewable*

Want to edit the link in some way, such as change its name or delete it? No problem. Right-click on the link and you get a dialog box allowing various operations on the selected link:

- Edit source

- Make default

- Remove source

- Choose thumbnail

- Add to favorites

Video

Let's explore Videos. You'll find the option on Kodi's main menu (Figure 8-15).

Figure 8-15. *Video selected on Kodi's main screen by hovering the cursor over it*

A number of video-related icons appear, the number varying as you add or remove video sources and playlists. Media sources include those you create, just as we linked to picture sources in the previous section. There's a lot of duplication on this screen; basically, these are just handy shortcuts.

Adding Video Resources

Adding a video resource is slightly different in the way we start it but then exactly the same as we did in creating picture resources earlier. Here, instead of clicking on Video, move the cursor over Files on the top row of icons and click it. You'll get a similar menu (see Figure 8-16) but with video sources and other video-related items. Click Add Videos and, again, it's the same from here in creating a video resource.

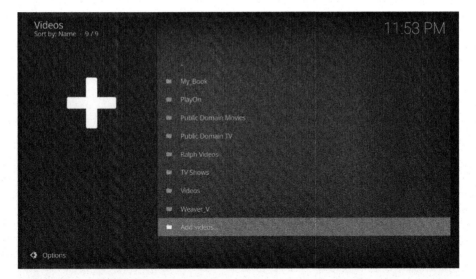

Figure 8-16. *The Files menu for Video*

TV Shows and Videos are directories on the Raspberry Pi's microSD, card and my strong recommendation is not to use them for media storage. Especially not for video file storage, as they often run into the gigabytes in size and can eat all the space on the microSD card in no time at all. Everything else is a resource link I've added to my system.

The last line, also like the Add Photos screen we've already met, is for adding resources—in this case, of course, video resources.

Click on it, and then click the Browse button on the dialog box that pops up. We now have the same list of protocols, as you can see in Figure 8-17.

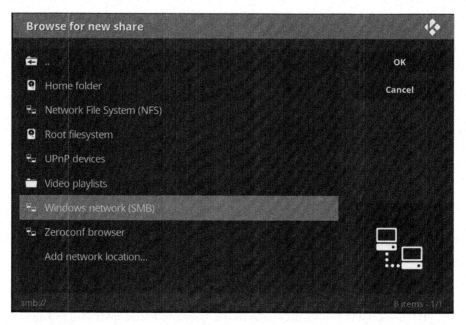

Figure 8-17. Adding a video resoure (or music) is very much the same technique as adding picture resources

We'll look at video playlists shortly, but first let's finish out the Video main menu selection with add-ons. You add video sources using the same method by which we added picture sources previously. The results are different only in that they are added to the Video menu instead of the Pictures menu.

Here's the method for adding a video resource link, again (like Pictures) using linking to a directory on a Windows computer as the example:

1. Click on a network protocol or location on the list in Figure 8-17.

2. Choose a computer on your network and navigate to the directory desired or other location such as an Internet website.

3. Click the OK button on the right, and the Browse for new share menu goes away, leaving the Add Video source dialog box. Click the Add button, and then OK, and you're finished.

Return to the Video menu (in Figure 8-16 earlier), and we find the new link. It's permanent and ready to use. If you want to edit or remove it, right-click on the name and a dialog box including those choices pops up.

Video Add-ons

Now, let's look at video add-ons. Go to `Add-ons` ➤ `Download` (clicking on both) and we get the screen shown in Figure 8-18.

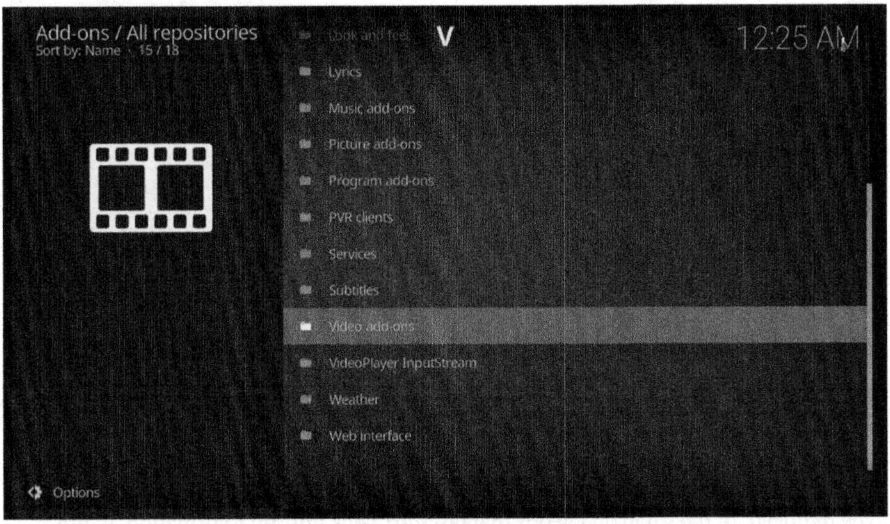

Figure 8-18. *Click on the Video Add-ons menu to add third-party video enhancements*

Click on `Video add-ons` to get a list of available third-party enhancements for Kodi (over 2200 on this list along). To install a video add-on, click on it and take these steps:

1. On the add-on information screen that comes up, click on `Install`.

2. Wait for the add-on to download, install, and enable (usually only a few seconds).

3. Return to the Video Add-ons menu.

Your add-on is now listed. Click on it to use it. As an example (Figure 8-19), I've added a selection of how to paint videos by Bob Ross (a fixture of classic TV; even if you don't want to paint, these shows are often mesmerizing).

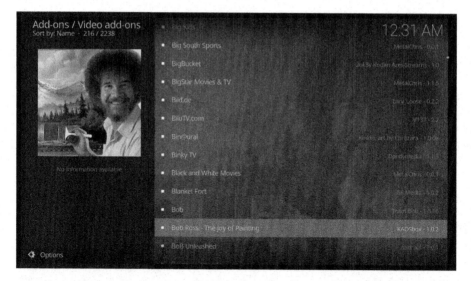

Figure 8-19. *The add-on for watching Bob Ross show us how to paint*

Should you not like an add-on and decide to remove it, there are three ways to do that. First, go to Video ➤ Video - Add ons and right-click on the title of the add-on to be removed. In the small dialog box that pops up, click Add-on Information. In the information screen concerning the add-on, choose Uninstall.

Video Playlists

Playlists contain links to media files, which are played in a specified or randomized order. Kodi offers us two types of playlists—basic and smart. You can have these playlists in both Videos and Music.

Basic Playlists

Basic playlists are nothing more than regular text files. You can either create your own using Kodi's built-in playlist editors (there's one for basic and one for smart playlists) or get pre-made playlists from other sources.

Let's make a basic playlist from scratch. In my case, I have a directory on the 4TB drive attached to my Raspberry Pi media controller. By the way, one of the many good things I'm getting out of writing this book (and passing along to you kind folk) is the knowledge of how one builds a powerful home theater using RPi/LibreELEC/Kodi. That is a winning combination, and I'm keeping mine.

Anyway, on the attached hard drive I have a folder in which I'm accumulating some of the many videos I've made. I like showing them off to visitors, and what better way than to have a playlist showing them in the background with low volume. A playlist for ease of accomplishing this demo of my production ability is in order. We'll use my construction of that playlist as an example.

The first step is to make a link to the resource, in my case a directory on the attached hard drive called, appropriately enough, Videos. We've used this technique in the "Pictures" section earlier in this chapter, and it works the same way here and in Music as well. Here we go:

1.   Navigate to Videos ➤ Files.

2.   Click on Add videos.

3.   The Add Video source screen comes up; click the blue Browse button.

4.   On the resulting Browse for new share screen, click on the method required for getting to your source—since my hard drive is connected directly to the RPi via a USB hub, I choose Root file system, then Media.

5.   In my case the 4TB My Book drive is now listed. So I click on it and a directory appears.

6.   Now move down the directories to Videos (that's what I want to use in building my playlist).

7.   Click on Videos—we get a blank listing, but that's fine at this point Click the OK button.

8.   We find ourselves back on the Add Video source screen, but the path to our video source is now listed.

9.   At the bottom of the screen, edit the name of the link (I'm calling this one Ralph Videos) and click OK.

10. A Set content dialog box appears. I'm accepting the default values, so we just click OK again.

That's it. We find ourselves where we started, on the Video - Files screen, but now there's a new link—Ralph Videos (Figure 8-20).

Figure 8-20. *We've created a new video resources link, Ralph Videos*

Well, that is a handy shortcut, and we can right-click on it and tell it to play the videos on the directory. However, it's still not a playlist. Let's now make a playlist from this resource link.

Click the Ralph Videos link. The directory listing for my Videos directory on the big hard drive comes up (see Figure 8-21).

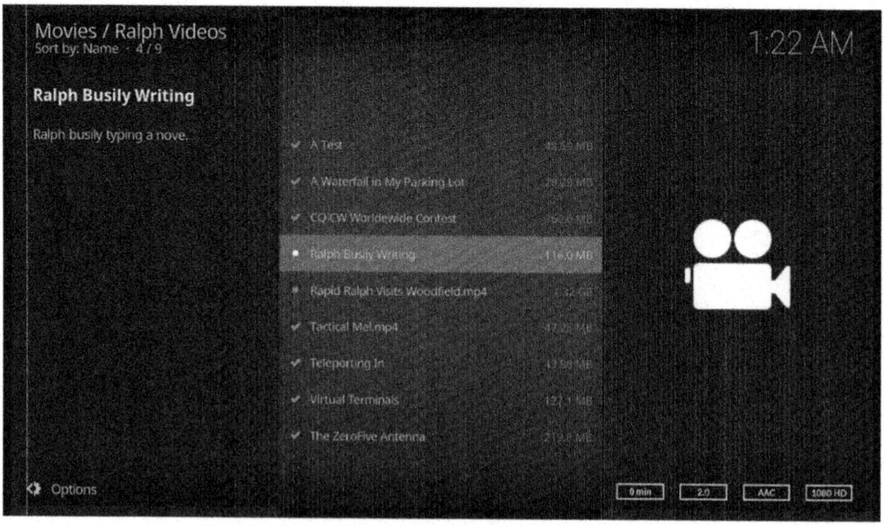

Figure 8-21. *Videos currently in this video resource link*

Good. All the videos I've copied into that directory are there. Now it's time to build the playlist. Here's how simple it is from this point:

1. Right-click the top video and choose Play from here.

2. Stop the video (click the square stop button at the bottom or press Esc on a keyboard twice).

3. Slide your cursor over to the left side of the screen to activate the side options menu and click Go to playlist.

4. Verify that all the videos in the directory are now in the queue (they are; see Figure 8-22).

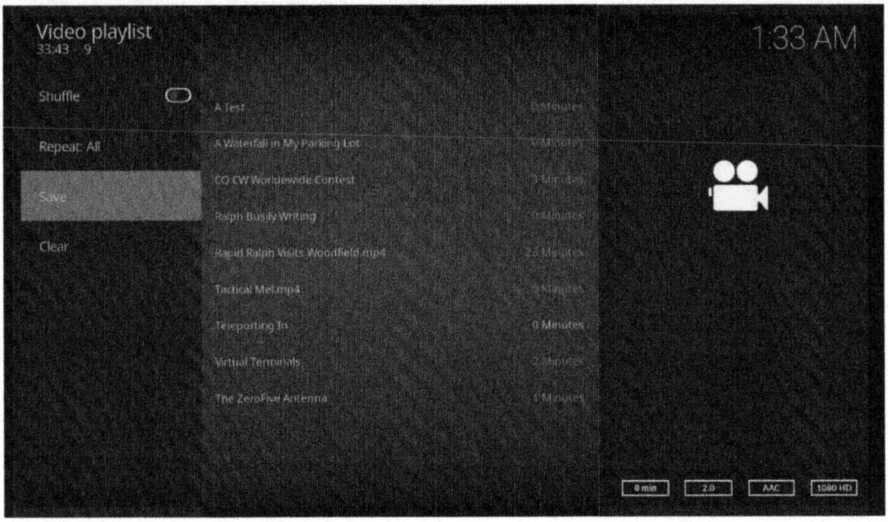

Figure 8-22. *The playlist menu*

5. The playlist menu has now changed. We'll select Repeat all so that the playlist will continuously play all videos in the directory—a good idea for a background video display, the purpose of this playlist.

6. Now click on Save and we're done.

Go back to Kodi's main screen, click Videos ➤ Playlists, and you'll see that our playlist now appears (Figure 8-23).

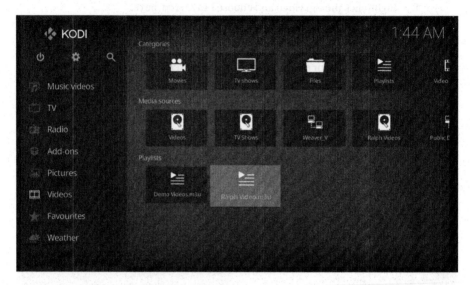

Figure 8-23. *The new playlist is now listed*

To use this basic playlist, right-click it, and a screen showing titles in that directory pops up. Click Play and we're off to the races.

There are also two other kinds of playlists in Kodi—Party playlists and Smart playlists. Playlists in Pictures, Music, and Videos all are created and used in the same way. In fact, you can even make playlists that mix media together.

What We Learned

This extensive chapter has devoted considerable space to Pictures and Video. You've learned how to create links to resources, resources being nothing more than collections of media files. Using Kodi, you can link to sources on the microSD card (not recommended due to limited storage space), hard drives or other storage devices attached to the Raspberry Pi, drives or directories on other local computers on our home networks, or sources out on the Internet.

You also learned about the different protocols used to connect to other computers and the Internet, about all the many add-ons available, and side menus. We also constructed a basic playlist.

Now, on to music.

CHAPTER 9

■ ■ ■

A Musical Interlude with Kodi

One good thing about music, when it hits you, you feel no pain.

—Bob Marley

Music, when you think about it, makes up about seventy percent of entertainment. At least that's how the old cliché goes as I learned it years ago as a young sound guy. Some well-known movie producers have weighed in on this subject. George Lucas, Academy Award winning creator of *Star Wars*, has said it's fifty percent. Danny Boyle, director of *Trance* and other movies, says, "The truth is, for me, it's obvious that 70, 80 percent of a movie is sound," he says. "You don't realize it because you can't see it."

Movies, TV shows, video games all have soundtracks. Without music and sound effects, most visual entertainment would fall flat. Music, unlike these visual media, also stands on its own as relaxing or inspiring or get-up-and-dance entertainment. So, that's what this chapter is about—playing music on your home theater with the smart-controller enhancements you gain using a Raspberry Pi, LibreELEC, and our buddy Kodi.

Now, one further thought before we dive into the mastery of music via Kodi. You have noted by now that we're spending a lot of time exploring Kodi. Why? Because building your entertainment center is a one-time process, which does not take long at all. All the esoteric technical subjects we touch on later in the book will occupy little if any time for most of us. However, you will be using your home theater for countless hours of enjoyment and enlightenment. The more comfortable you become with Kodi, the more you'll get out of the extensive time you'll be spending using it to serve up whatever you feel like viewing or listening to at any given moment.

A Little Inspiration

This book prepares you for building, enhancing, and downright enjoying your own smart media center. I don't have room to cover every single feature or every detail in a Raspberry Pi/LibreELEC/Kodi–controlled media center. In the chapters so far and in those to come, you're getting a comprehensive foundation in constructing a media center. Like many projects, it looks complicated at first but as you preserve though all the details, it becomes easier. Thanks to Kodi, you'll have room to add features and obtain enjoyment in many years to come.

© Ralph Roberts 2017
R. Roberts, *Mastering Media with the Raspberry Pi*,
https://doi.org/10.1007/978-1-4842-2728-2_9

Years ago, I had a business partner. Whenever I'd have a brainstorm and suggest taking on some new project, he'd always ask, "Where's the pony in it?" Meaning, what would we get out of it, where's the reward?

It occurs to me that you kind folks reading this might like a little inspiration. Let's use my experience. In building my own media center from scratch to provide examples in this book, I had a sudden realization the other day. With not a whole lot of effort, my media center had involved into a quite pleasurable source of pure entertainment. Something I enjoyed watching movies on and listening to music.

In my case, I have a 42" flat-screen TV with built-in speakers and a DVD player attached. We could watch cable and play rental movies. Not much of a home theater. The popcorn my wife makes is good, but we couldn't stream digital music off the Internet, show my YouTube channel, hang big hard drives for storage off it, look at the many thousands of photos I've taken over the years (all digitized), or access all the music, video, and movies on my local network. Nor do all the hundreds of other things an intelligent media center controller provides.

In short, the old system was very two-dimensional in that it only did two things— show TV and play movies on DVD. After a while, boring.

Like, I'm sure, all of you, I wanted more. For an investment of under $100, I got it. In Figure 9-1 (case removed) is Sandy (network name), my Raspberry Pi/LibreELEC/Kodi media controller with a HifiBerry tophat 25-watts-per-channel amplifier. I'm listening to classic guitar music on it right now, streaming off the Internet, as I write. Good background music does wonders for concentration.

Figure 9-1. *My Raspberry Pi 3 running LibreELEC/Kodi with a HifiBerry Amp+ 25 watts-per-channel stereo amplifier board*

Now, why the amplifier? If you already have a wowser of a soundbar and/or surround sound speakers, use that. However, for the price of a Raspberry Pi Model 3 ($35) and the HifiBerry Amp+ ($59 on sale last Christmas), I saved a lot of money over purchasing a soundbar and so on. The RPi does a lot more.

By the way, it's always good to have spacers between the boards (white plastic tubes on each corner in Figure 9-1). They keep the boards from coming together and perhaps shorting out. Usually spacers come with the tophat board, but always install them.

Speakers? I used to be in the stereo business, so I've got lots of speakers. Should you get a tophat amplifier like mine (according to a support person at HifiBerry), you can use any 4–8 ohm rated speaker with the Amp+. He says this won't damage the Amp+. You should, he adds, select the speakers not by power rating, but listen to different speakers and choose the pair that sounds best for you. As a long-time stereo aficionado and professional sound guy, I echo that (pun, as ever, intended). He also said the power output is about 45 W peak power into 4 Ohm at 18 V. At lower voltages and higher loudspeaker impedances it is less.

Plug the Amp+ into the Raspberry Pi (it works fine with Kodi), do a tiny bit of configuration, hook up the speakers (see the HifiBerry website), and you've got high end audio for not only the TV but any other sound source you want to hook up to your media center.

There's a pretty good selection of sound boards out there, so shop around; I'm not endorsing any product. Features you're looking for (and I've got) are these points from the HifiBerry Amp+ specs (from the HifiBerry website):

- Up to 25W output power

- Capable of driving 4 Ohm speakers (also works with higher impedance speakers)

- Fully controllable from the Raspberry Pi

- 44.1kHz and 48kHz sample rates

- Digital-analog conversion included—no need for external DACs or sound cards

- Fully digital sound path for optimal audio performance

- Connects directly to the Raspberry Pi—no additional cables needed

- Only one 12-18 V external power supply needed for both AMP and the Raspberry Pi—no need for USB power supply anymore5W output power

- Only one 12-18 V external power supply needed for both AMP and the Raspberry Pi—no need for USB power supply anymore

Returning to the exploration of Kodi now in progress, let's look at the Music selection on Kodi's main screen.

The 25 watts per channel output (left and right stereo) fills up a room nicely.

Also, even if you already have a great sound system on your TV, the Amp+ or similar board allows running speaker wire to speakers in another room or out on the patio. Play music for summer cookouts or whatever.

So, there's the pony for me and, I think, you as well. The RPi/LibreELEC/Kodi intelligent music center solution provides a center for growth, variety, and fun.

Now, we return to exploring Kodi, still in progress. Specifically, the Music selection on Kodi's main menu bar.

Music

Move the cursor over it and you'll see it turn blue (in the Estuary theme) indicating selection of the menu item, as shown in Figure 9-2.

Figure 9-2. The Music main menu item turns blue when selected

Navigating Music

You'll find navigating in Music very much the same as we did in Pictures and Video. In the interest of completeness, it's good to mention here—helping you understand why Kodi is the way it is—the unique history of Kodi again. This is because, while it is being smoothed out more and more with each new version, Kodi started in an unusual manner.

Kodi was first known as XBMC, that acronym meaning Xbox Media Center. Xbox is a registered trademark of Microsoft, covering that company's popular line of video game consoles. The first Xbox came out in 2001. XBMC, quite amazingly in its time converted an Xbox to a media center for the playing of music and videos. Version 1.0.0 of XBMC debuted in 2004.

The first Xbox consoles, harking back over 13 years now, were quite limited in memory, processor speed, storage, and all the great advances we've been gifted with over the past decade and more. Not the least of which include systems on a chip, the Raspberry Pi itself, and much faster hardware overall. The later generations of XBMC/ Kodi, as it was ported to (converted to run on) more powerful systems, suffered some from design compromises owing to the limits of its first home on early Xboxes.

This is not to say that XBMC, now renamed Kodi, hasn't made great strides in updating its software to take advantage of newer computer architectures, especially (in our interest here) single-board computers like the Raspberry Pi. Kodi remains the best all-around choice for building an RPi-powered media center. I'm just mentioning that some quirks still exist, although fewer with each new version, which brings us to navigating Kodi's Music selection on the main menu.

One of those quirks concerns how choices work on the main menu bar. A lot of modern programs feature hierarchical (often called "tree") menus—meaning you click on the main menu and get a list of items and/or submenus; click on a submenu and get a list of that submenu's items and/or sub-submenus. Kodi 17 is indeed closer to being a true tree menu.

Kodi 16's main menu items were different in that by simply moving a cursor over—for example here, Music—two submenus appear, Files and Add ons. OK, that's the classical upside-down or tree menu, right? But, wait, there's more. Clicking on Music (or Videos or Pictures, and so on) also brings up a menu. If that sounds confusing, it was.

Kodi 17 makes it easier for us, with the Music main menu selection being among the choices on the right of the main screen (see Figure 9-2 for how this looks).

Now, here's where version 17 is a bit tricky. Moving the cursor over Music selects it (turns blue in the Estuary skin). You'll see a group of tabs at the top for submenus and (if your library is populated) rows of album covers or other artwork. Click on Music and a list of selections appears, *but* the submenu tabs are gone! The submenus look like Figure 9-3.

Figure 9-3. Submenu tabs for Music

Only four of the Music submenu icons appear here, but there are actually thirteen. Use your mouse cursor without clicking to do horizontal scrolling for accessing all of them, or the arrows on your keyboard, or the same arrows on a remote control device.

Most of these submenus require you to have albums, songs, and so on added to Kodi's music library, which we'll do in the next chapter. Here's what they do:

> Genres: Presents a list of music sorted by genres such as rock, classic, country, and many more.

> Artists: Lists music alphabetically by artist.

> Albums: The names of albums in the library appear on this submenu's list.

> Singles: Lists music released as single songs.

> Songs: Lists all songs alphabetically (or however you sort and/ or filter them using the Options menu at the bottom left of the screen).

Years: Lists music by the year published.

Top 100: Lists music in your library on Top 100 lists.

Recently added albums: Lists your more recent album downloads added to the music library.

Recently played albums: Lists the albums you've listened to recently.

Playlists: Shows the playlists of music you've programmed.

Roles: This submenu has submenus of its own, where you can generate lists by roles such as conductors, album artist, contributors, and so on.

Files: You can also get to files in Addons ➤ Music. This is where you add music resources for importing into the library, playlists, and so forth.

Music add-ons: Provides a shortcut to the Add-ons ➤ Music area.

Kodi finds the information above in various databases on the Internet. Let's make some music now.

Making a Simple Playlist

We begin with these steps:

1. Move the cursor over Music (or otherwise select it with a remote).

2. Without clicking, move the cursor to the Playlist selection on the row of Music submenus we met earlier.

3. Click on Playlist.

The screen changes and the submenu menu appears (see Figure 9-4) with choices for creating three types of playlists.

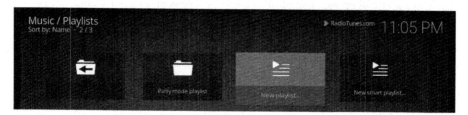

Figure 9-4. The three types of playlists

Creation of music playlists uses the same process. In fact, you can mix media into your playlists, presenting photos, music, and videos in whatever order pleases you, creating neat multimedia experiences to entertain yourself and your friends or any other group.

Click Playlists. The resulting choices are

1. Party mode playlist

2. New playlist

3. New smart playlist

See Figure 9-4 again for how they look.

Again, constructing a music playlist is the same procedure we used in making basic picture and video playlists. Since we're now going to do an example of a simple playlist, we will skip a couple of steps. We could do it through the Playlist submenu described earlier, and that would be fine for a party mode or smart playlist, but those require a populated music library. We don't do that until the next chapter. So we'll do this the easy way.

1. Navigate to Music ➤ Playlists and click Files.

2. At the bottom of the Files list, click Add more.

3. Click Browse for new share screen, and click on the method required for getting to your source.

4. Choose the directory, drive, or link for the music files to be added.

5. Click on Music, and click OK.

6. We find ourselves back on the Add Music source screen with the path to our music source now listed.

7. At the bottom of the screen, edit the name of the link to whatever you want.

8. A Set content dialog box appears; click OK again.

That's it, we find ourselves where we started, on the Music ➤ Files screen, but now there's a new choice—your new basic playlist. It's ready for use; just click on it.

Now let's finish learning our navigation of the Music selection on the main menu bar.

Clicking on Files

Go back to the main screen and select Music again by moving the cursor over it. Move the cursor over to the Files submenu and click. We now have the Music ➤ Files screen, as shown in Figure 9-5.

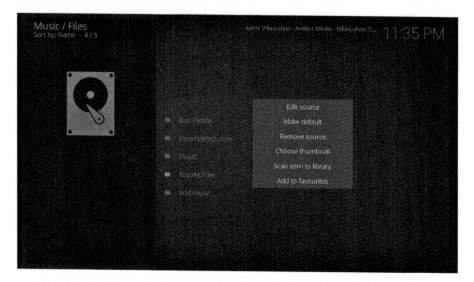

Figure 9-5. *The Music ➤ Library ➤ Files screen*

On a newly installed version of Kodi, this screen will have only two choices, Music and Add music. But this version of Kodi is my personal entertainment center, being built as I write this book. So, as will happen on your own, I've started adding items. My_Books, as you will recall, links to the 4TB storage hard drive added to my Raspberry Pi 3. Royalty Free is a basic playlist where I have tons of music used as background music in the documentaries produced by my video company. In time, you and I will all have pages upon pages of sources and playlists.

The bottom menu item, Add music, lets us create basic playlists (as we did earlier and in Chapter 8).

I've right-clicked on a music source, bringing up a dialog box showing some of the choices associated with creating and maintaining libraries. Kodi's libraries , as we will see beginning in the next chapter, give us powerful methods for finding, linking, and constructing extensive libraries of our favorite music or movies or photographs/other graphics.

Clicking on Add-ons

Choosing Add ons ➤ Music, as we did in both Pictures and Video, gives us access to third-party scripts that program additional features into Kodi. Figure 9-6 shows my active add-ons. in I have Kodi playing background music during my writing work days most of the time. Good music helps me concentrate and come up with good words.

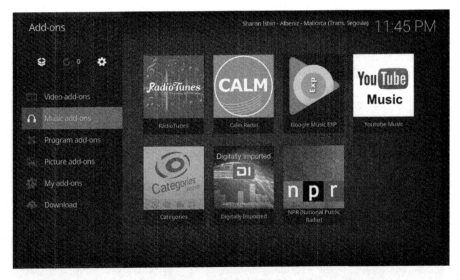

Figure 9-6. Clicking on Add ons ➤ Music displays the current active add-ons

The musical selection (classic guitar) listed just to the left of the time in Figure 9-6 is the background music playing as I write. Good stuff to write by. To get more music add-ons, go to My Add-ons on the main menu and click on Music, as in Figure 9-7.

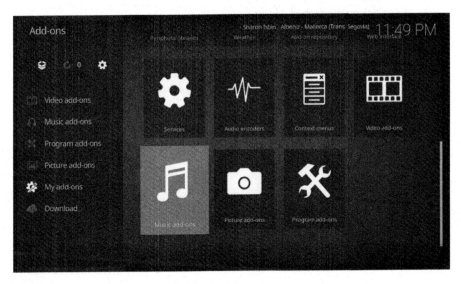

Figure 9-7. Finding additional add-ons for Music

Figure 9-8 shows how your selection might look.

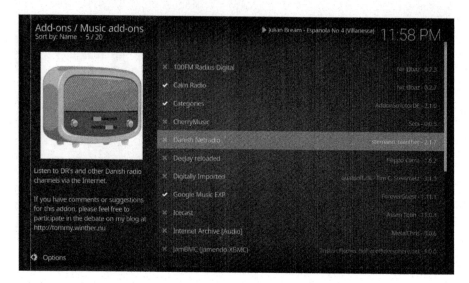

Figure 9-8. *Selecting new music-relating add-ons*

To install:

1. Click on the desired add-on.

2. On the resulting dialog box, click on Install.

Now when you go back to the Music ➤ Add-ons screen, you'll find the new add-on there, as in Figure 9-9 (top). Just click on it and, in this case, it brings up a list of available Danish radio stations (Figure 9-9, bottom). Click one of those and listen live.

Figure 9-9. *Click on the new add-on to activate it*

To remove an add-on, got to the Available add-ons menu, find the add-on and right-click on it, and then right-click Information. A dialog box with an uninstall selection appears.

A general comment. Kodi, from its origins as software running on Xbox game consoles, sometimes works a little different than expected, as in the earlier example. The way you truly learn Kodi or any software's hidden goodies, eccentricities, and (most of all) the many good tasks it can accomplish for you is simply to play with it. Explore it, experiment with its features, and soon you'll find it a lot easier to use. This book gives you a good start toward mastering your Kodi-driven media center, customize it to your liking, and obtain many hours of entertainment from it.

What We Learned

First of all came an inspirational example about the "pony" that's in constructing and adding the features we want to an RPi/LibreELEC/Kodi media center. Which is to say, the reward for creating such an inexpensive yet powerful combination is a powerful home theater good for untold hundreds of hours of entertainment.

We then explored the Music selection on Kodi's main menu. We mastered how to scroll horizontally through the submenus, constructed a simple playlist, and learned how to find and install third-party music-related add-ons. Now, let's move on to Kodi's music library.

CHAPTER 10

■ ■ ■

Music Libraries

What in the world would we do without our libraries?

—Katharine Hepburn

Most recently—in Chapters 7, 8, and 9—we've looked how to use the three major media groups. Pictures, video, and music comprise those things we'll be viewing or listening to for general entertainment. We now have explored the menus, learned how to add sources for those three groups. This includes how basic playlists get constructed and the installation of add-ons for obtaining more media files than is on our local media center or on other computers connected to our home networks.

Wow! Lots of stuff, huh?

No.

Out on the Internet exist millions (literally) of songs, movies, cat photos, and so on. A vast wonderland of about any kind of entertainment we might be in the mood for listening or viewing.

Can we download everything that strikes our fancy and play it on our home theater whenever we like?

No. You'd need a hard drive the size of California.

Ah, but what we can do is catalog whatever sources we want on the Internet and browse our catalogs to find whatever we like. *Then* stream music, video, and pictures off the Internet until 3 a.m. despite the necessity of being at school or work the next morning. Yeah, I've done that a few times. Makes life fun.

Of course, how the heck do we keep track of thousands of media files with enough information such as thumbnail photos, actors or musicians involved, genre, and so on? Why, we'd need a database of some kind, hopefully one that would automatically load all this data and keep track of it. Something we could browse and select items to play with ease.

Right, libraries.

Libraries

A *library* in Kodi denotes one of the built-in databases. The two most used are the Music Library and the Video Library. These databases are standard SQL (Structured Query Language) databases, just like those running web sites and providing all sorts of online information. They have a small memory footprint but can handle those thousands upon thousands of media sources you'll want to accumulate and (very important) find easily again.

© Ralph Roberts 2017
R. Roberts, *Mastering Media with the Raspberry Pi*,
https://doi.org/10.1007/978-1-4842-2728-2_10

On the http://kodi.wiki site (a Wikipedia-like site devoted to the Kodi software) these two libraries are defined like this:

- **Music Library**: Kodi collects ID tag information to create the music library, and scrape metadata from the Internet.

- **Video Library**: Kodi scrapes information from external websites to create the video library.

The term *scrapes* refers to automatically copying titles, posters, covers, artists, and other information about each media file you'll be streaming from a particular site. This data is often called *metadata*. We'll learn how to load up your music and video libraries in this chapter and scrape the needed metadata into them automatically linked to the correct music or video or, yes, music video (Kodi's set up to handle those as well).

Copyrighted Material

Before getting to linking and scraping, let's address the elephant in the room, that being copyrighted information.

Content owners want to protect (that is, get paid for or maintain control by preventing others from using it without permission) their copyrighted material. In the United States, the federal government backs them with the Digital Millennium Copyright Act (DMCA). As stated in the Wikipedia: "This copyright law, based on international treaties, "criminalizes production and dissemination of technology, devices, or services intended to circumvent measures (commonly known as digital rights management or DRM) that control access to copyrighted works. It also criminalizes the act of circumventing an access control, whether or not there is actual infringement of copyright itself."

To break that down into plain English:

1. It's against the law to break DRM and distribute pirated works.

2. It's against the law for you or me to watch or listen to pirated works.

So, because a myriad of third-party add-ons allow access to, for example, every episode and every season of popular TV shows or recently run movies or the latest music from major bands, does that make Kodi illegal? No. It's add-ons that allow downloading or streamed of pirated shows and music that are the problem. The ones you can add using the Video Add ons or Music Add ons have been vetted and are OK. They provide public domain media or free usage with ads. It's the unofficial add-ons from other sources you have to worry about.

Can you get into trouble not paying in some manner for copyrighted works? Maybe. For instance, according to media reports, in 2015 the cable giant Comcast started sending out warning notices to Kodi users. Comcast does not monitor your usage, but various content owners do. If they get your IP address and complain to your Internet provider, a legal hassle can ensue.

Downloading hundreds of TV shows and movies and/or thousands of songs is so easy in this day of fast Internet that we all want to build immense libraries. Kodi allows you to do that; just exercise good sense in doing it, especially if you have a public IP address (as most of us do).

That said, on to the good stuff.

Music Library

You will truly like this! Kodi does most of the work involved in adding music to the Music Library. We start with a music source—that being songs or other music media you've downloaded or link to via the Internet for streaming.

Streaming music or video, of course, means you play it from the Internet without having to store it on your local system. This means you can have truly massive libraries, far more than all the available space on all the hard drives on all of your computers. Is that cool or what? Excitingly obvious answer. Bigger is better.

A starting point is downloading music with metadata (titles, cover art, artists, and so on, also called music *tagging*) in a format Kodi can recognize. Many sites have this already. For example, music you've bought from iTunes, Google Music, or similar services has that information and, since you have already paid for its usage, you can legally add it to your Kodi music library to easily find and play it whenever you like.

Here are the basics of using such data.

Music Tagging

I need to stress something very important about tagging here. Kodi adds music into the library by scanning each file for such standard data tags as artist, album title, cover artwork, titles of songs in the album, year of release, genre, and so forth.

Kodi scans media files and stores this information in the database (the music library) along with links to where the music file exists. This latter, the location of the music, can be on hard disks or other media attached to your Raspberry Pi or somewhere reachable on your local network. Or it can be a source accessible on the web and which can be streamed by Kodi. We can sum up the broad categories of music sources this way:

- On your media center computer (a Raspberry Pi in our case) or a hard disk attached to the media center

- On CDs/DVDs played from drives attached to the media center

- On hard drives, CD/DVDs, USB media, and so on available through your local network or from devices connected directly to your Raspberry Pi

- Streamed from the Internet

The advantages of having music links to these sources scanned into the library are many, including:

- Efficient management of your collection

- Grouping of music by genre, artist, record label, or any other criteria for which tags exist

- Creation of smart playlists and party mode presentations

- Display of album covers, photos of the musicians, and so on

- Easy searching for songs you're in the mood to hear

- Much more

Getting music into the library is easy enough and essentially automatic once Kodi is instructed to scan a source containing music files. However, there's a rub. If the media file does not have tags, Kodi cannot add it into the library. It will, however, still link to the music but will not show in the library. Nor will it show up in library searches.

So, yes, tags are critically important for library inclusion, but what if you want an untagged music file loaded into the library?

Tagging Untagged Media Files

The Kodi wiki site, http://kodi.wiki, strongly states the importance of tags:

> *"Your audio files MUST have correct audio tags to use the Music Library mode. Without tags you're limited to the file view in Kodi."*

Adding tag data to your music files is called *scraping*. Kodi pulls information from tagging services, "scraping" it off the Internet. To set up scraping, click on the Settings icon at the top left of Kodi's main screen, then on Media settings, then Music, then Library, and then Music. This screen is shown in Figure 10-1 for your reference. If you're familiar with previous versions of Kodi, this is a little different but accomplishes the same end result—configuring Kodi to scrape data for music and video from the Internet.

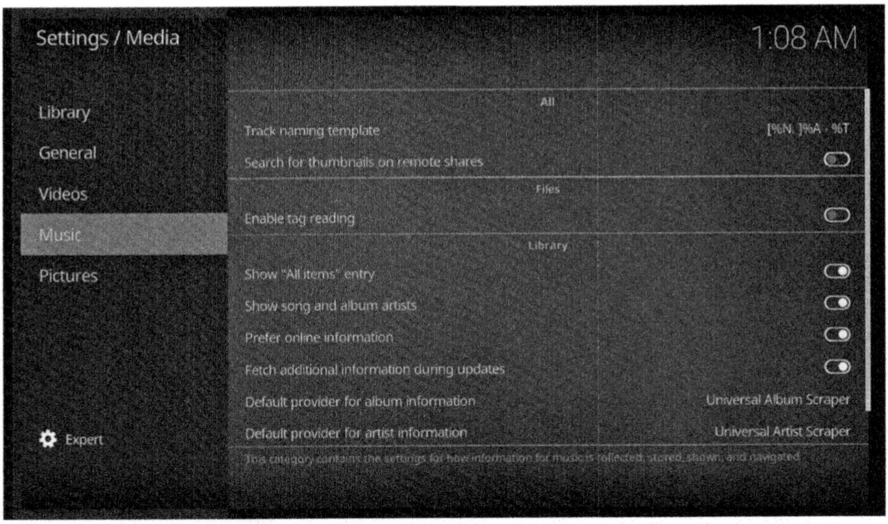

Figure 10-1. *Music library configuration screen*

Configure these settings as in Figure 10-1, assuming you want automating scraping of data to occur. Basically this involves turning on all the selections in the Library section on the screen. This enables Kodi to add tags so that library entries happen. Explanations follow on what these configuration choices accomplish so you can choose what you want.

Fetch Additional Information During Updates

Turn this section on and Kodi searches for additional tags (called metadata) from online sites. The Kodi wiki site recommends turning this selection on. As they state: "Since we are a media center and this kind of stuff is great, we recommend you turn this option on. It will download lots of things with scrapers such as artist biographies, moods, artist thumbnails, album artwork etc."

A disadvantage to the earlier suggestion lies in the fact that a large music collection requires extra time to achieve finding and scraping in the additional tags. Also, if some of your files are not properly tagged, some may wind up with erroneous data attached. So, decide what you want here, as well. The next item can help you overcome errors in tagging.

Prefer Online Information

This configuration replaces some of the artist and album tags with data scraped offline. Since the scraper sources Kodi recommends are reasonably accurate, it can fix a lot of tagging problems. I need to emphasize here that scraping data only changes the tags, not the actual music. Also, you can manually edit tags for individual songs or albums if found to be incorrect. I recommend you turn this on. One of joys of using a media center is having all this descriptive data available when deciding your next listening or viewing pleasure.

Scraper Selection

These two configuration items allow the selection of a scraper to pull in the data described earlier. Kodi employs two scrapers. One downloads and attaches data including artist biographies. The other grabs associated artwork such as album covers and photos of musicians but also album descriptive text, genre info, and reviews. The Kodi wiki sums it up: "We recommend you stick with the Universal scraper here, which will use the MusicBrainz API to search and a number of different sites such as Fanart.tv, TheAudioDB.com and Allmusic to grab the additional data. Since some of these sites are open, it is possible to add information to these sites and scrape the new data from them instantly." This action is most easily done on another computer and saved to whatever media used with the Raspberry Pi. However, there are web browser add-ons which would let you access the web directly from Kodi.

I agree, having checked out and played with MusicBrainz and looked at the other sites, with Kodi. MusicBrainz is free; check it out at https://musicbrainz.org/. To use MusicBrainz on your own computer you'll need their free downloadable software installed on your computer. Look under Products on the MusicBrainz web site, choose Music Picard (named after the Star Trek face-planting captain, I believe) and follow its installation instructions. See http://kodi.wiki/view/Music 20tagging for how to use it in editing your tags. This link also provides additional info on the settings in Figure 10-1.

Next, I'll show you how to get many hundreds of cool, legal-to-use, music files to jump-start your music library.

Downloading Free Music

A major source for public domain and music/videos otherwise free to use is http://archive.org. There are millions of musical selections, millions of movies and other videos, millions of TV shows, millions of books (you can read ebooks on Kodi), *billions* of web pages, and so on.

As to the web pages, check out the Wayback Machine. It chronicles the Internet! It even has one of my first websites from December 19, 1996 (I've been on the web for a long time). Figure 10-2 shows some of the info on Archive.org 's first page.

Internet Archive is a non-profit library of millions of free books, movies, software, music, websites, and more.

| 284B | 12M | 3.2M | 3.4M | 1.4M | 166K | 1.4M | 175K | 252K |

Q Search   GO

Advanced Search

Figure 10-2. *The Internet Archive (http://archive.org) is a fantastic source of legal to use music, video, and more*

Let's get some contemporary tunes with the standard album/title/artist and so forth format that Kodi will understand and automatically add to your library. If you already have some either on an attached hard drive to your Raspberry Pi or on a computer on the local network, you're good to go. However, in the interest of completeness, I'll show you the whole process.

First, I go tune hunting and download some tunes to one of my computers. We'll use the Internet Archive as a starting point. I went to the main page at http://archive.org and scrolled down looking for music sources. One source caught my eye, Netlabels (Figure 10-3).

Figure 10-3. *Some of the media libraries available on the Internet Archive*

Opening Netlabels yielded a goodly selection of music legal to download. Bad Panda (Figure 10-4) seemed like an excellent starting point (who doesn't like pandas, eh?).

Figure 10-4. *A legal to download record label under Netlabels is Bad Panda*

In case your initial viewing looks different, Figure 10-4 shows the Thumbnail view—the default view shows a list. . Anyway, I opened Bad Panda, listened to some of the music, liked it, and downloaded a bunch of tunes. Figure 10-5 shows a sampling of choices on this label.

Figure 10-5. *Some of the albums free to download from Bad Panda*

To download one of these or other media files from the Internet Archive, use this procedure:

1. Click on the title.

2. On the next page, look at the download options and click on
    VBR MP3.

3. One or more files appear. Move the cursor over each one, and
    a small downward arrow appears.

4. Right-click on the file title and select Save Link As.

5. This brings up a standard file-handling dialog box on your
    computer. Choose a destination directory and click Save to
    start the file downloading.

The result was a directory on my computer entitled, appropriately enough, "Bad Panda." It looks like Figure 10-6. The important thing to note is the presence of metadata (titles, art, and so on). You'll find more of that revealed after importing this music into Kodi's music library.

Figure 10-6. Files in a music source directory now on my local network

135

Importing into Kodi's Music Library

Now, we'll get your (or anybody's) music sources into the library. First, either move the storage device from the other computer to the RPi or put them on a network that the RPi can access. Now use the following steps to import into Kodi's Music library:

1. Click Music on Kodi's main menu.

2. Click on Files.

3. At the bottom of the Files menu, select Add Music.

4. The Music Sources dialog box appears. Click Browse and navigate to the directory where your new music files are located.

5. Click on the source directory.

We're now in the directory, but you see no files listed. Don't worry; we're just here for the link. Click OK and you see the dialog box shown in Figure 10-7.

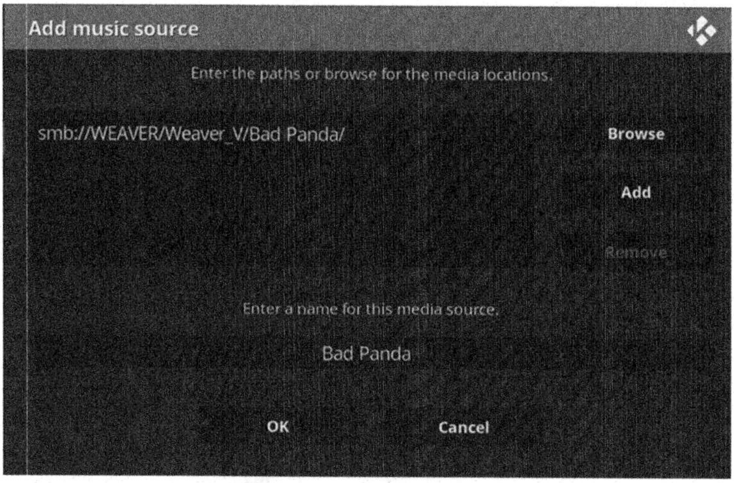

Figure 10-7. *Music source directory selected for addition to library*

One important thing to note about the Add Music source box. It now has the path to your music source. In my case, the directory is on my work computer, Weaver (I name all my computers), on its Weaver_V drive, and the name of the directory is Bad Panda. To record the location of all this music into the library database, check the name (you can edit it if you like), and then click OK at the bottom.

Data about all the music you downloaded into the source directory now loads into the library. Wait until it finishes. A line at the top shows the file processing, and this operation may take a bit of time if you have lots of music.

That's it. What, you expected complexity? Nah. Adding sources is this easy. In a moment, you'll see how directly link to sources on the Internet but first, our reward. Go back to Kodi's main screen and move the cursor over Music. As shown in Figure 10-8, we now have music!

Figure 10-8. Now that the music library has data in it, more tabs appear under Music

Click on Music and then Albums, and a list of albums appears (Figure 10-9). Click on any one to see and play the music in that album.

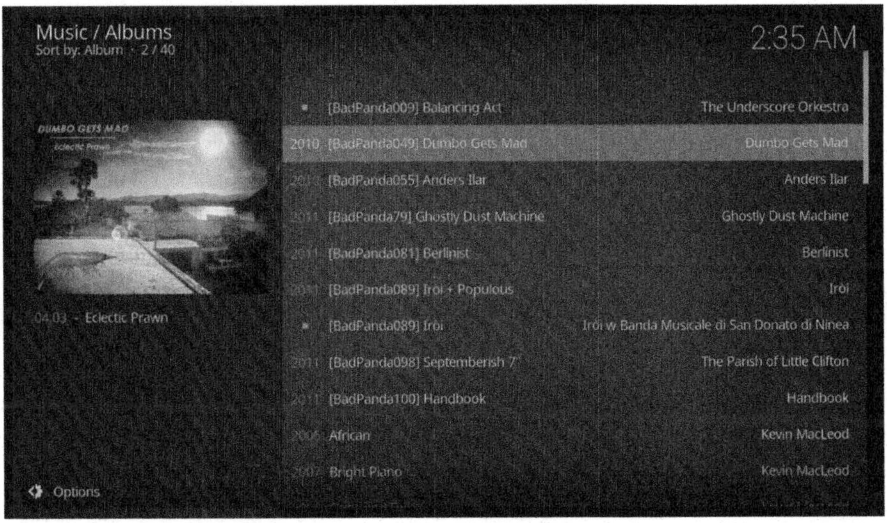

Figure 10-9. List of available albums in the music library

Once you've started a song playing, go back to Kodi's main menu. The active media file (in this case a song) shows its title next to the time in the upper right on Kodi's various screens. You can do other things in Kodi while music plays in the background. To stop or pause the music, you need to access the options/sidebar menu shown in Figure 10-10.

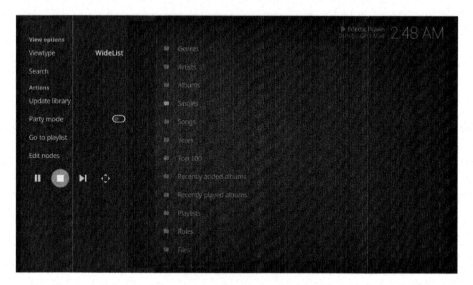

Figure 10-10. *The current media selection playing appears on Kodi's main screen with a control panel to pause, play, dismiss it, and so on*

To stop music, use the small control icons at the bottom of the menu. The first icon pauses, the second stops, the third moves to the end of the current selection, and the diamond-shaped icon expands the music selection into a full-screen view with additional controls (see Figure 10-11).

Figure 10-11. *Full-screen view of music currently playing*

The music you now have in that music source has been moved into the library, and you can add other sources in the same manner. However, if you're like me, you'll be finding other pieces of music and downloading those as well. Obviously, then, updating Kodi's music library is necessary.

Move the cursor over Music and click it, bring up the options/sidebar menu by moving your cursor all the way to the left side of the screen or by clicking Options at the lower left, and select Update library. If you have a lot of music, this updating requires time.

Adding Streaming Sources from the Web

No matter how many hard drives you have, they won't be as big as the Internet. Literally billions of media files live out there, just waiting for you to listen and/or view them. There's no way any of us could store all that. The answer is to stream the files from the Internet to your system.

Streaming media are music or video files received by your system from an online provider, shown to you as the sound or picture arrives but not permanently saved to your computer drive. The great advantage of this is the ability to watch large files, such as the several gigabytes of a feature movie, without having to devote storage space to it.

Getting streaming media into your library—that is, a link to it and metadata stored— is not easy. If it's a live stream, for example, it will be gone after the event is over and no way to link to it. However, recorded media like record albums, movies, TV shows can be linked to and, if allowed, entered into your libraries (music and video).

The easiest way of obtaining streams is through add-ons. You can get add-ons that supply access to thousands of radio stations, huge libraries of music, thousands of movies and TV shows, and so on. But add-ons mostly come from independent third-party developers, which the folks who program Kodi have no control over. Many third-party

139

add-ons protect their copyrighted material by not permitting downloads or linking such as putting it in your library. In short, you can listen or watch but not download (they're afraid you might sell copies or some such).

The way to tell if you can get, in this case, music into your library from an add-on is simply by right-clicking (or highlighting if you're using a remote) on the item/items you want. If the context menu includes Scan item to library, you're good to go. Otherwise, there are ways to link to the item or add it as a favorite.

What We Learned

In this chapter, you learned the basics of Kodi's powerful library features. We set up music resources and scanned them into the library and saw how the Music selection on Kodi's main menu gained extra tabs such as Albums and Artists. We also saw that tagging data must be attached to any media file before the library can scan it in, although it does add a link in Files. Additionally, tags can be added to files that don't have such data through scraping; that is, the downloading of titles, artists, cover artwork, and the like from the Internet.

Next, put some popcorn in the microwave—we're going to the movies, especially those in our video libraries.

■ ■ ■

CHAPTER 11

Video Libraries and Other Sources

People who LIKE movies have a favorite. People who LOVE movies couldn't possibly choose

—Nicole Yatsonsky

Is the popcorn ready? Time to watch movies and other videos the smart way, using Kodi's video library.

Like the music library we met in the preceding chapter, the video library makes collecting, finding, and viewing movies smart and enjoyable. As with music, extra material is stored along with the link to the video source containing the movie. Lists of actors, movie posters, genre, reviews, plots, and other data enhance the process of finding a movie to watch.

The Video Library

As with importing music, adding movies/videos to the library requires tags. To utilize all the library power in Kodi, some sort of data must be present. If such metadata does not exist, the library does not see (pun, as ever, intended) the video. All is not lost if a movie you want to watch is not in the library. You can still find and view untagged media files; it's just more cumbersome. This assumes that the file is visible to Kodi, previously linked by you. Here are three ways of easily finding non-library files to view:

- Find it in the Files lists; for movies or videos go to Videos ➤ Files.

- Access a basic playlist containing the file.

- Have it bookmarked as a favorite (access using the star icon on Kodi's main screen).

Now let's move on to loading the library with movies and so forth.

© Ralph Roberts 2017
R. Roberts, *Mastering Media with the Raspberry Pi*,
https://doi.org/10.1007/978-1-4842-2728-2_11

Importing Movies and Other Videos

The procedure for getting video into Kodi's video library is generally akin to the way we added music to the music database in Chapter 10. Let's get some movies into our databases.

Naturally, we need a source. In my case, I like old movies and collect them. We discussed the Internet Archive (http://archive.org) in the last chapter. It's a good place to download public domain (no longer under copyright) movies from, as is https://free-classic-movies.com/. Between the two of them, I've been filling up a directory entitled (rather appropriately) Public Domain Movies. Figure 11-1 shows what it looks like so far.

Figure 11-1. *Collection of classic movies ready for adding to Kodi's video library*

Creating a Video Source

Your collection(s) of movies can reside on directories on any of these:

- The SD card in your Raspberry Pi (not recommended, too slow and not enough storage space for a decent-sized collection)

- A hard drive or DVD drive attached to the RPi

- A hard drive anywhere on your local network

- A cloud service out on the Internet such as Google Drive, OneDrive, or similar

- Other sources on the Internet allowing linking and streaming movies

Using my classic movie collection as an example, we'll use the following procedure in adding them to Kodi's video library. First, turn the directory they reside in to a video source in Kodi:

1. Move the cursor over Video on Kodi's main menu.

2. Click the Files icon in the main part of the screen.

3. At the bottom of the Files menu, select Add videos.

4. The Video Sources dialog box appears; click .Browse and navigate to the directory where your files are located.

5. Click .the source directory and enter it.

In this example, the public domain movie directory is on the V: drive of a computer on the local network. We're now in the directory, but you see no files listed. Don't worry; we're just here for the link. Click OK and the dialog box shown in Figure 11-2 appears.

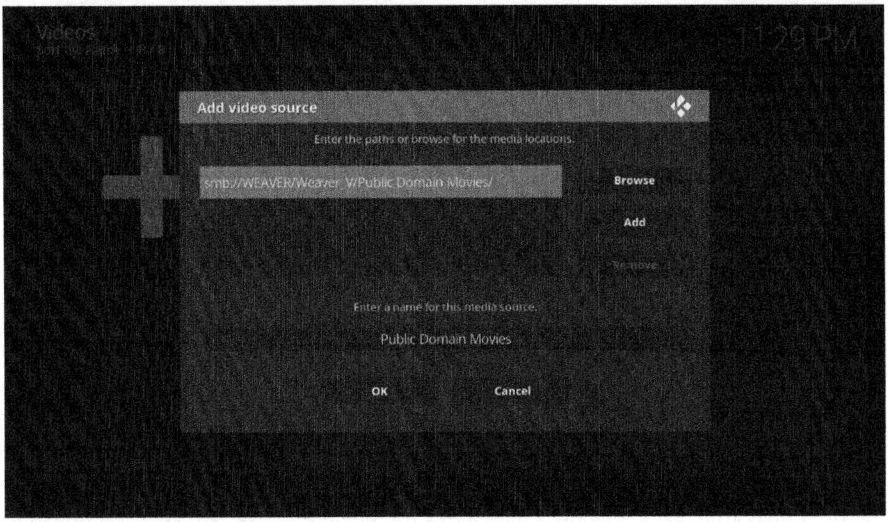

Figure 11-2. Creating a link to a directory containing download movies

Your next step is to edit the name in the Edit a name for this media source box. Change it to something that makes sense to you. In my case, this source directory contains public domain movies, so I entered Public Domain Movies. Perhaps not highly original, but I'll know what's there when I see this link in Kodi's Video / Files submenu.

143

After editing, click OK at the bottom of the screen. The link is now complete. Go to Videos ➤ Files and you'll see it listed there, as on my system in Figure 11-3.

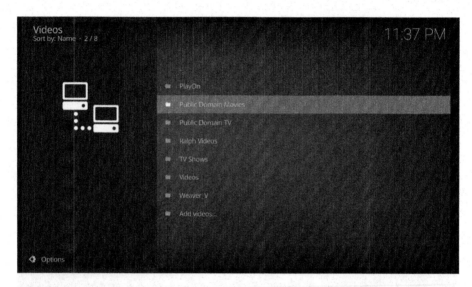

Figure 11-3. *Links to video sources appear in the Video ➤ Files submenu*

At this point, your video and/or movie source link is just that, only a link. Click it (left-click if using a mouse), and the directory on the device where the movies are stored will open and show a listing of the movie files. While you can click on a title and play the movie, it's not in the video library yet. However, you can set up basic playlists of selected movies or even have Kodi play them all in sequence. Nice, but nothing approaching the power of the video library database.

Before we get to automatically entering all the metadata—titles, actors, plots, reviews, background information, and so on—look at the listing of your movies. When you open the source directory, a small icon showing the movie poster appears (if that information is attached to the movie file). Click the side menu (the tab at the left side of the Estuary screen) and then Big List at the top. The list changes to large icons showing movie posters. Very colorful and certainly useful in selecting a movie to watch. Still, we can do a lot better than this.

In my public domain movie source, there are already well over a hundred movies, and I am constantly finding and downloading others from the Web. Kodi's video library now links to all these movies and contains metadata for each one. Again, it's necessary to emphasize, a movie must have metadata attached before the library will enter it.

If you have or will occasionally download movies that do not have metadata information, it can be added later. Also, after finding and downloading movies to an existing video source, Kodi scans the new flicks into the video database.

Scraping Metadata

Before you scan the first time, it's necessary to set the scraper. Scrapers we met in Chapter 10— they're add-ons allowing Kodi to reach out on the Internet and download metadata for each title being scanned into the database. This is how Kodi adds all the movie posters, lists of actors, reviews, and so forth to each movie link. You obviously want a different scraper for movie posters than album covers, that is, for music than for movies or TV shows.

To set the scraper for movies, right-click the title of the video source on the Video ➤ Files screen. As shown in Figure 11-3, we use my Public Domain Movies source as an example. In the resulting dialog box, click the Change Content item, and the box shown in Figure 11-4 appears.

First thing, and it's important, under the This directory contains line (see Figure 11-4), set the content type (use the arrow buttons) to Movies, as shown. Other choices are TV shows, Music videos, and None. Each of these allows for categorizing the type of media into an appropriate database, making managing the material much easier. It also provides the right database fields for recording the kind of metadata normally attached to the category, such as actors, plots, posters, and the other items downloaded with or scraped from the web for movies.

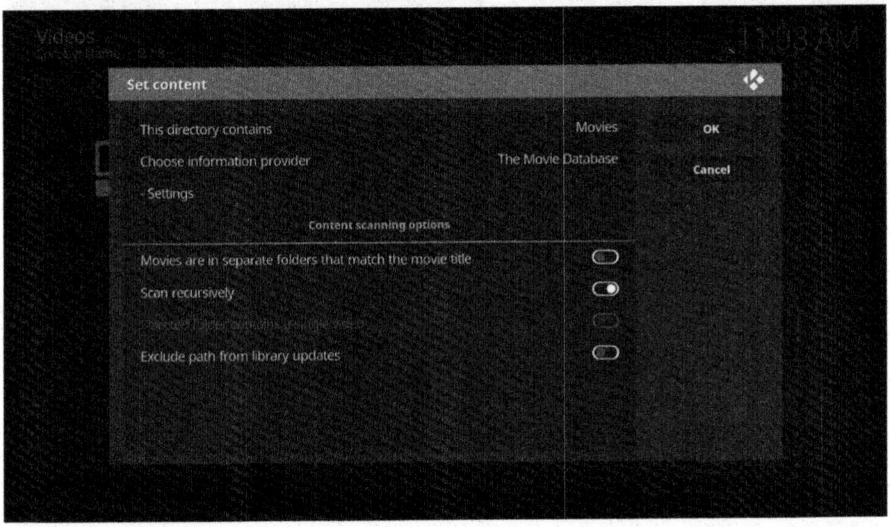

Figure 11-4. Kodi includes the Movie Database Scraper by default, as shown here next to Choose information provider

As shown in Figure 11-4, the Movie Database Scraper, which Kodi includes in its basic installation package, appears by default in a new installation. If your movies are subdirectories, click Select Scan recursively if your directory contains movies in subdirectories so that the scan process finds all films. Then click the X in the upper right of the box to collapse it and continue. Note that there is a Kodi icon in the extreme upper right of the Set Content dialog box. Moving the cursor over it causes the X to appear. Left-click to close the box.

145

However, should you want to try other scrapers, click the current scraper line (Choose information provider). The next dialog box shows your installed scrapers. Click Get more, and the screen in Figure 11-5, full of other scrapers, comes up. Move the cursor over the titles. Click on the scraper's title to install it. You can install as many as you like. Also note that many more scrapers are available through other repositories (see Addons ➤ Download add-ons to install additional repositories and other add-ons).

Figure 11-5. Additional scrapers are available

Scanning Content into the Video Library

Now we execute the procedure for getting a video source into the library. In Figure 11-6, I've right-clicked Public Domain Movies. A dialog box pops up. We want the bottommost choice, Scan for new content. This same procedure works for manually updating the database after new titles have been added to the source.

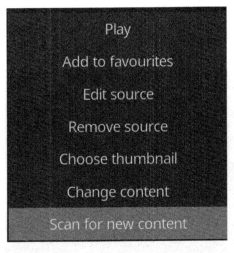

Figure 11-6. *Scan for new content adds tagged movies to the video library*

Depending on how many movies are in the source directory, it takes a little time for Kodi to scan and enter data into the database, so wait a few seconds if need be. Again, Kodi captures the data and links the movies. The movie files, often a gigabyte or more in size, remain in the source directory.

After successfully adding movies to the database for the first time, you will note changes on Kodi's main screen, as shown in Figure 11-7. There are now movie thumbnail posters on the main screen!

Figure 11-7. *Movie selections appear after the video library becomes active*

147

The Movies dialog and several icons appear above the posters, as we see in Figure 11-8. The tabs allow sorting by Sets, Title, Genres, and so on, which all give us different methods of exploring Kodi's video database.

Figure 11-8. *The video database groups movies by genres as guided from data scraped from the Internet when the movie was scanned in*

Click Genre, for example, and Kodi presents a list of various genres. Choose one of those and get a list of corresponding movies in alphabetical order. The video database, by the way, contains information about all the movies from all the video sources you've scanned into the video database. It's possible to have many thousands of movies; hence all these database features become quite important in finding the films and/or types of films you want to watch.

Clicking Movies (highlighted in Figure 11-7 earlier) produces an alphabetical listing of the movies in the Video database. Moving the cursor over titles causes information about that movie to appear.

Looking at this title from my collection in Figure 11-9, peruse my collection and it quickly becomes obvious that I love old westerns and cheesy sci-fi flicks, among others. As we scroll down the list, Kodi shows us the posters from each movie. Here, "The Cowboy from Sundown" is highlighted. (Tex Ritter was a famous singing cowboy and country music star. He was the father of actor John Ritter).

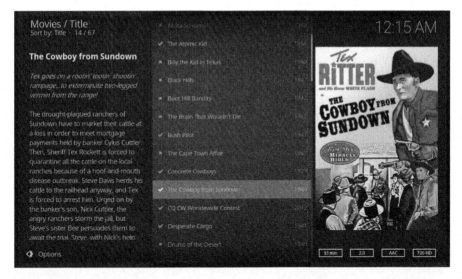

Figure 11-9. *Scrolling aphabetically through your movie collection brings up data about each movie; this info was scraped from the Internet when we scanned the directory your movies are in earlier*

Clicking a selected title tells Kodi to play the movie, as we see in Figure 11-10.

Figure 11-10. *Select a title and click to play the movie*

Seeing Metadata

In addition to these methods of looking for movies, check out the Options menu. It allows you to really dig into the database for addition information or to narrow down searches. To access the Movies version of this menu, just move the cursor over the word Options at the bottom left of the Movies screen and click, or move the cursor all the way to the left edge of the screen, and the menu pops up. While using the Estuary theme, it looks like Figure 11-11.

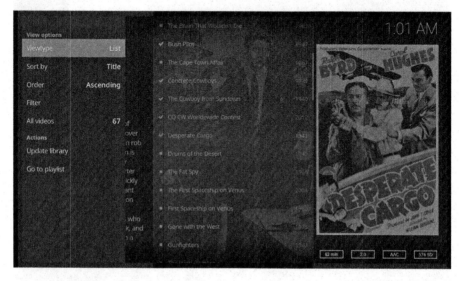

Figure 11-11. *The options or side menu while in the Movies menu tree provides powerful methods of viewing, sorting, filtering, updating, and using playlists*

Check out the View selection first. Clicking it rotates you through seven choices, enabling you to better find and select movies for viewing. You can change the view as much as you like by causing the side menu to slide out and clicking around through the views. Whichever movie title the database is currently on will be reflected in these different views. Very cool and useful. Here are the seven views:

1. **List**: Shows an alphabetical list of movie titles with (if present) a movie poster for each title as you slide the cursor over it, as in Figure 11-9.

2. **Poster**: Presents a horizontally scrolling line of poster thumbnails with each poster enlarging and descriptive information of the movie appearing when the cursor passes over its thumbnail (click a poster as always to play that movie).

3. **Shift**: Also horizontal moving thumbnails but with information above the line of movies and no enlargement of posters.

4.   **InfoWall**: Alphabetical list of titles with information and posters appearing on the left as the cursor passes over each title.

5.   **Widelist**: Same as InfoWall but the list is wider.

6.   **Wall**: Has rows of thumbnails with no information; click a thumbnail to play that movie, as shown in Figure 11-12.

Figure 11-12. *Wall view lets you choose movies from a thumbnail posters*

7.   **Fanart**: Shows a list of titles on the left with "fanart" (drawings or photos submitted by fans) on the right (Figure 11-13).

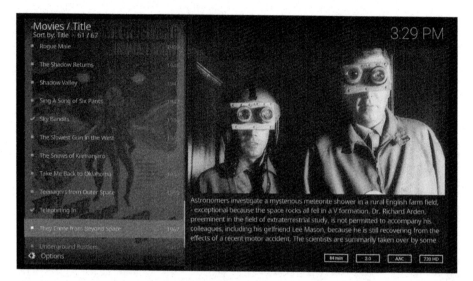

Figure 11-13. *Viewing fanart makes browsing though the video database fun*

The seven views in this first selection in the options/side menu (Figure 11-11 earlier) provide handy tools for making the choice of the evening's movie viewing easily, but there's more.

- **Sort**: The second selection allows the sorting of movies rather than just going down the list alphabetically. With hundreds of movies in your video database, alphabetical might become tedious. We also have eight option here which allow sorting by title alphabetically, by year made, by rating, by your rating (yes, you get to rate movies after watching), by MPAA rating (Motion Picture Association of America), duration, date added to database, and the play count (how many times you have watched it).

- **Order**: The third selection line lets us sort from A–Z or Z–A. Is that popcorn ready yet?

- **Filter**: The fourth line allows filtering of movies; that is instructing Kodi to list only a certain category of movies. Click Filter to active this feature, and then Misc options to choose filtering criteria. You can filter by title, rating, in progress, year made, tags, genre, actor, and director.

- The fifth selection provides for toggling on or off the hiding of titles you've already watched. Clicking on it rotates its title through All videos, Watched, and Unwatched.

- **Search**: enables finding a specific movie if you already know the title. Clicking Actions (below the menu selection) offers choices for narrowing the search.

- **Update library**: (warning, warning) causes the video and music libraries to update; that is, scan all sources for new media files. This can take a long time depending on how many sources are linked to the libraries. Do this only when you plan on going to the store for more popcorn. If you don't want to wait, click that line again and the scanning stops.

- **Current playlist**: yes, the current playlist (if one is active) is shown and gives you commands to shuffle or otherwise manipulate it. (We'll get back to setting up smart and party playlists shortly. We can do that now that you've got working video and music databases to support those types of playlists; the basic playlist works fine without databases, just not as powerfully.)

Manually Adding and Editing Metadata

We now have an idea how nice it is to have a video database chock full of movies. Once again, because it's all-important and worth repeating, for a movie to be listed in the database requires metadata attached. Once more, metadata are fields of data about the movie. Titles, actors, plot, reviews, format, length, ratings, posters, fanart (photos or art related to the movie), and more are all metadata. The amount and completeness of metadata varies but movie to movie but can be added or corrected later.

Metadata is obtained automatically, if you've selected a scraper as we did earlier in this chapter. It's powerful and wonderful; there's lots of good material about each of your movies. Unfortunately, the process is not totally perfect. If the database has errors, the scraper faithfully downloads those errors. You may, for instance, wind up with foreign language metadata or the wrong poster or nothing at all.

In the latter case, no data found, Kodi will not automatically add that movie into the database, as we found out earlier (however, you can do it manually as we shall see shortly). Kodi does give you access to individual movies in Library ➤ Files under Video, and you can add metadata manually or use a different scraper to find posters and the like. More about adding in a moment.

Editing Metadata

Should incorrect metadata be present after the movie has been scanned into the library, you can edit it. Let's look at correcting existing data first. In Figure 11-14, the metadata is right except that the title is in German (look at the bottommost title).

Figure 11-14. *The title is in German for this movie in both the list and the description*

That title—*Der schweigende Stern*—translates as "The Silent Star." Totally different than the American version.

Figure 11-15 shows how you edit a title. Right-click the title and select Manage in the dialog box (the bottom selection). The next box, Edit title, allows us to make our correction. Click Done and you are finished.

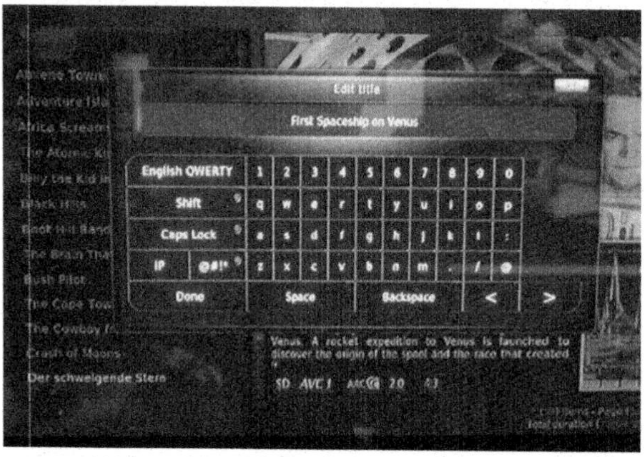

Figure 11-15. *Editing the title*

In Figure 11-16, the correct title now shows both in the list of titles and in the description. Perfect.

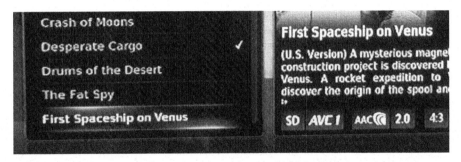

Figure 11-16. Title now shows correctly in both list and description

Editing Metadata

Let's assume you've downloaded a movie to a video source directory on a drive attached to your Raspberry Pi or to in a directory linked to by Kodi. Scanning that directory for content causes Kodi to look in the directory for metadata files or, if it doesn't find them, use a scraper to search databases on the Internet for posters, fanart, and so on. Sometimes—thankfully not often—the scraping process retrieves erroneous information.

As we just saw, Kodi gives us a way of editing titles. However, for other changes and fixes to metadata, we must edit the data from *outside* Kodi. Software called *library managers*, exist and are listed at http://kodi.wiki/view/Library_managers. Due to complexity and the state of support, I am not recommending any. It's easier and faster to extract the data already in the movie or other database in Kodi, edit the record you want to fix, and read it back in.

Fixing metadata is necessary only if it bothers you. For example, if the title or description's in a foreign language, that's worth editing just for your future ease of knowing what the movie is when browsing titles in your collection. If misspellings or other typos bother you, fix them or leave in place. It's your collection, add or ignore whatever you like.

So, here's how we edit.

During scanning movies (or any media file) into a database, Kodi creates an .nfo text file. The .nfo file extension has the same title as the movie it contains information for recorded in XML (Extensible Markup Language). Titles of and locations for graphics files such as movie posters and fanart are also present in the file.

First, we'll need to export the .nfo files from Kodi.

Most likely, you won't see this the first time you look at the directory but, rather, only the downloaded movie files. Thus, to edit metadata files we must first pull them out of Kodi and into the video source directory. Here's how to do that in Kodi:

1. Go to System ➤ Video ➤ Library.

2. Scroll down the list and select Export video library.

3. Click Separate.

4. In the next dialog box, click Yes or No for exporting the fanart and poster thumbnails (the four files shown earlier).

5. There are two more choices to make, actor pictures and overwrite old files.

The .nfo files, fanart, and posters for *all* the movies in the database now download to the appropriate source directories. Yes, it can take some time but you'll be set up to edit metadata as you find things to change for various movies.

These files look like this partial capture:

```
<?xml version="1.0" encoding="UTF-8" standalone="yes" ?>
<movie>
    <title>Africa Screams</title>
    <originaltitle>Africa Screams</originaltitle>
    <rating>6.500000</rating>
    <userrating>0</userrating>
    <epbookmark>0.000000</epbookmark>
    <year>1949</year>
    <top250>0</top250>
    <votes>2,929</votes>
    <outline>Abbott &amp; Costello search for diamonds in Africa, along the
    way meeting a visually-impaired gunner, a hungry lion, and a tribe of
    cannibals...</outline>
    <plot>When bookseller Buzz cons Diana into thinking fellow bookseller
    Stanley knows a great deal about Africa they are abducted and ordered
    to lead Diana and her henchmen to an African tribe. After encounters
    with lion tamers, giant apes and a wild river, Buzz returns to America.
    Stanley finds diamonds and buys the store they once worked for, hiring
    Buzz as its elevator operator.</plot>
```

We can edit the .nfo file for that title and correct or add metadata.

To accomplish this, we must have access to the file. The format of this file is exact, you must color inside the lines—in other words, don't mess up the format or the data won't read back into Kodi properly. Again, this information is in XML, which is a markup language using tags that represent fields in our movie, TV, or music Kodi databases. For example, look at the plot for this Abbott and Costello movie. It's text between two tags, <plot> and </plot>. The first tag represents the name of the database field and the second denotes the end of text in the field.

No problem if you make a mistake and the data for that movie looks jumbled. Just edit the .nfo file again and reload.

Before editing a movie's .nfo file you first must find it. Look in your video source directory, that is the place on your network where you download the movie you want to fix. Mine happens to be on a Windows 10 computer and, with the large icons options selected, a movie file with metadata files looks like Figure 11-17.

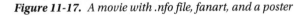

Northwest-Trail-1945.mp4   Northwest-Trail-1945.nfo   Northwest-Trail-1945-fanart.jpg   Northwest-Trail-1945-poster.jpg

Figure 11-17. *A movie with .nfo file, fanart, and a poster*

Here, we have the movie file, the .nfo file, fanart, and a poster. In addition to editing the .nfo file, you can change the fanart and poster thumbnail files—just maintain the naming conventions so that they will group together in the database.

Simple is best when selecting software to edit .nfo files. Free doesn't hurt either; you do not need a fancy, expensive program editor. If you have a Windows computer on your network, the answer is *Notepad*. Notepad, a basic text editor, comes with Windows and is uniquely suited for this task.

The major requirement in editing these files for an editor is ability to read and save UTF-8 characters. The Wikipedia defines UTF-8 as:

> *"...a character encoding capable of encoding all possible characters, or code points, defined by Unicode and originally designed by Ken Thompson and Rob Pike. ... The name is derived from Unicode (or Universal Coded Character Set) Transformation Format – 8-bit."*

This is important, as most text editing software uses ANSI character encoding (American National Standards Institute). ANSI and UTF-8 are schemes for extending the basic ASCII (American Standard Code for Information Interchange) characters used by early computers. However, we need not swim further in an ocean of acronyms—just remember; .nfo files require UTF-8 character encoding.

How do we get that? Notepad, for example, opens using ANSI by default. Here are the steps:

1. Open Notepad and navigate to the directory linked to by Kodi as a video source (or if not local network, move the storage device attached to your RPi to the computer used for editing temporarily).

2. In File name (second line from bottom), enter ***nfo**. The asterisk (*) is a wildcard character showing all .info files to be listed. This instructs Notepad to show those files only. Hit Enter. You get a blank screen as Notepad is still set to look for text files using ANSI character encoding.

3. In the drop-down Encoding menu (bottom line of Notepad screen) choose, that's right, UTF-8, and all the .nfo files exported out of Kodi appear as shown in Figure 11-18.

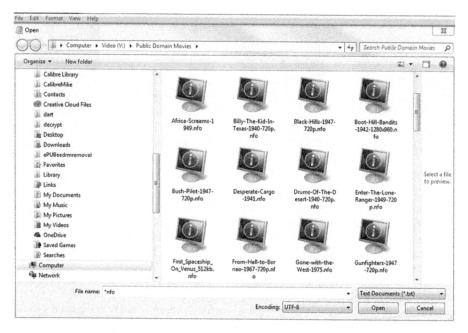

Figure 11-18. *Select UTF-8 in to see and edit UTF-8 files*

We are now ready to open and edit the .nfo file. That file, of course, consists of the fields in Kodi's database record for a movie, album, or TV show and exported in XML format. I've picked "Africa Screams," starring those hilarious classic comedians Abbot and Costello. As you can see in Figure 11-19, there's *lots* of metadata for this movie. Most will not have this much.

When Notepad loads the file, the lines do not break, and some of the information will be off the screen. To fix this, click Format on the top menu bar and then choose Word Wrap. Now you can see the entire record, and nothing is affected (you can read the file back into Kodi without turning off Word Wrap).

Figure 11-19. *Most movies don't have this much metadata, but more is better*

158

By the way, a jumbled mess like Figure 11-19 is hard to read. Feel free to put line returns after closing tags (like `</plot>`) and even blank lines to isolate the field or fields you want to edit. Kodi does not care, and it will make your editing more convenient.

Now, we can edit. As a test, I made a minor change in the `<outline>` field. After the names of the two main characters, Buzz and Stanley, I added who played them in parenthesizes—Bud Abbott and Lou Costello, respectively. Changes complete, it's time to get the modified record back into Kodi (if you moved the storage device, reattach it to the Raspberry Pi now).

Here's the easiest and fastest method:

1. From Kodi's main menu screen, go to `Movies ➤ Titles`.

2. Find the title for the movie you just modified and right-click.

3. Left-click `Movie information`.

4. At the bottom of the information screen, click `Refresh` and choose `Local` instead of `Internet`.

That's it. A bonus is, now that you've exported all those `.nfo` files into your source directories, correcting errors is easy whenever you like.

Adding Metadata

What if a movie or other media file *does not* have an `.nfo` file with it, and nothing can be scraped from the Internet? Kodi has you covered! This technique will be especially appropriate, for example, in adding home movies to the video database. It's most likely that your home movies do not have existing metadata on the Web. Scrapers come up with nothing.

So, to add a home movie or any other movie/video, TV show, or music file, just create an `.nfo` file with the exact name of that media file. Let's say you have a video titled `visiting aunt flo.mp4`. In the same directory, create a file named `visiting aunt flo.nfo`. This is a critical requirement; the names must match exactly except for the extensions. Also, these files should be in a directory you've already set up as a video source in Kodi.

In creating and editing this file, you'll need an editor that recognizes and saves UTF-8, such as Notepad, which we used in editing existing `.nfo` files earlier. We also need a simple template to set up metadata acceptable to Kodi. Here's one I use with only title, sort title, genre (grouping types of videos helps in finding them), and a description in the `<outline>` field.

```xml
<?xml version="1.0" encoding="utf-8"?>
   <movie>
        <title>Some title</title>
        <sorttitle>It will sort by this title if you include it</sorttitle>
        <genre>HomeMovies</genre>
        <outline>put a description here</outline>
   </movie>
```

Your edited file might look like:

```xml
<?xml version="1.0" encoding="utf-8"?>
    <movie>
        <title>Visiting Aunt Flo</title>
        <sorttitle>Visiting Aunt Flo</sorttitle>
        <genre>HomeMovies</genre>
        <outline>It was a long drive but we made it in time for supper. This
        video shows the tasty meatloaf supper Aunt Flo made and Bobby's
        birthcake she had made for him. Great visit!</outline>
    </movie>
```

Kodi allows a limited way of adding more tags. An effortless way is to look in an .nfo file scraped from the web for one of your movies and use those tags. For more info on editing and using tags, check http://kodi.wiki/view/NFO_files/Movies#Video_.nfo_Files_containing_XML_data on the Kodi wiki.

Custom tags can be anything you want to keep track of in your movie collection not already provided. As an example, perhaps <my_opinion> </my_opinion>, where you can your feelings about the movie for your own use.

To add your own custom tag(s), do this:

1. Go to Videos ➤ Library ➤ Movies /Tags.

2. Click New tags.

3. Type in the name of the tag.

4. Click Done.

5. Choose the movies you wish the tag to apply to, by holding down the Shift key and clicking each title (I did say it was limited).

At any time, you can navigate to Videos ➤ Library ➤ Movies ➤ Tags and change or delete tags. Use your custom tags in the same way as existing tags in .nfo files. That is, <yourtag> ... some text ... </yourtag>. The information in tag (the new database field you've created) will show up in the movie information for the movies you designated.

In editing .nfo files, remember to stay within the tags, the file must be properly formatted for Kodi to read and translate it correctly into the database. If the metadata for a movie in Kodi is garbled after pulling it back into Kodi, no problem. Check your file and correct any format errors, typos, and so on. Then read it in again.

Reading the new home movie or whatever into the database, now that we have an associated .nfo file (remember, the same exact name as the video) is accomplished like a little differently than refreshing a modified listing.

First, of course, this is a new listing so it needs scanning in a special manner. Here's how we do it:

1. In Video / Files, right-click the video source your new video is in.

2. Click Change content.

3. Select Local information only.

4. Make sure Movies is selected under This directory contains.

5. Click OK.

6. Again, right-click on the video source directory name and then click Scan for new content.

Your new video should now be listed in the movie database.

The TV Shows Database

Building a TV show database uses essentially the same techniques as we did earlier. One difference is the necessity of telling Kodi the video source we're linking to contains TV shows. It's a simple change:

1. In Video ➤ Files, right-click the video source containing TV shows.

2. Click Change content.

3. In This directory contains, select TV shows.

4. Now choose the TVDB as the scraper to pick up TV show metadata from the web.

5. Click OK.

Here's where it gets a little more complex than entering movies into the movies database. The TV database is set up for series, since most TV shows have seasons and episodes within each season. So, naming conventions for titles are all important.

Here's an example. I like classic TV series—such as "The Beverly Hillbillies"—and decided to start adding them to my Kodi's TV show database. The first 55 episodes are in public domain now because the producers forgot to renew copyright. The setup is a minor effort but after that, to paraphrase Jed Clampett, they go in quicker than a fox into a henhouse.

First off (oops, now I'm writing like Jed talks), Kodi expects each series to have its own folder within the video source directory holding TV shows. Okay, easy. I created a folder named The Beverly Hillbillies. It's best to name folders the exact series title so that scraping works properly. Within a series folder, you can copy in files as you find downloadable episodes for the series you collect. However, and this is a big *however*, they must be renamed in a specific format so that Kodi knows what season and what episode each file contains.

Here's an example. I just downloaded an episode from season 1 entitled "Jed Buys Stock." Here is how the file is named:

```
TheBeverlyHillbillies105-JedBuysStock_512kb.mp4
```

Kodi cannot read that or scrape for additional information. Thus, before copying it into the series folder, a renaming must occur. The general format is simple once we find out what that might be. Here's the general convention:

```
anything_(s)eries#(e)pisode#ext
```

The anything here can be the episode title. Series number and episode number are obvious. The ext is the media file extension, such as .mp4, .mov. Which all translates, using the download title earlier, as:

```
Jed Buys Stock_s01e05.mp4
```

Copy this renamed file into the series folder and we are ready to head for Beverly Hills, lickety-split. Figure 11-20 shows how the episodes look in my Public Domain TV/Beverly Hills folder.

Figure 11-20. *The proper names for episodes in a TV series are all important*

By the way, certain other formats for episode naming work also. Refer to the Kodi wiki for those, but I suggest mastering this one first.

With TV shows properly named and in a series folder, we can let Kodi both enter them into the TV database and scrape the web for metadata. As with movies, go to Video / Files and right-click the TV source folder to be added. Click Scan for new content.

Clicking Titles, we find only one series listed but Kodi has scraped metadata for this series and each of the individual episodes (Figure 11-21).

Figure 11-21. *Just one series so far but metadata in place*

A tip for renaming TV show video files. Many great resources exist on the Web. For example, Wikipedia has articles on about every TV show you can think of, and these articles list seasons and episodes. This allows you to find the information you need to properly and enjoyably set up TV series the right way.

Another excellent resource is `http://thetvdb.com`. The TV Database site, as described on the site, "... is an open database that can be modified by anybody. Please click on login in the navigation to get an account. All content and images on the site have been contributed by our users, and are licensed under a Creative Commons Attribution-NonCommercial 4.0 International License."

Then there's the mother of all movie and TV databases, `http://imdb.com`. IMDB is the ultimate professional repository for data about movies and television. Owned by Amazon, IMDB is now the world's most popular and authoritative source for movie, TV and celebrity content. You can use the vast metadata riches of IMDB from within Kodi by installing and using the IMDB scraper (choose `Files` ➤ Video, right-click `Video Source`, click `Change content`, and then choose `Add more` under `Change scrapers`).

This is a good start for all of us in finding and downing episodes from TV series and putting them in place. For all the other things you can do in realizing the power of Kodi's TV database, check the wiki:

`http://kodi.wiki/view/Naming_video_files/TV_shows`

What We Learned

In this chapter, we learned about Kodi's video libraries and the requirement for metadata—titles, actors, plots, reviews, ratings, year, length, and all the other many facts about movies or TV shows—to be present before Kodi would link to a video file. We revisited the concept of scrapers, first met in the last chapter when used retrieving album covers, song titles, and so forth for music.

Scrapers, as we found out, are not always perfect. It's sometimes necessary for a little editing to correct errors or to add additional information you might come across. We met .nfo files and learned how to export them from Kodi and edit using WordPad while maintaining their UTF-8 character extension. Then you saw how to cause Kodi to read these files back into the database.

Of course, many video files do not have metadata on the web. We created .nfo files and you saw to attach them to a video file (by using the same name as the video file except for the extension). Instructing Kodi to use local information only, that is not to scrape web databases, we can now successfully add videos to Kodi's databases.

Finally, we delved into the TV database, becoming proficient in making series folders and renaming TV series episodes so that Kodi can tell and track their season and episode. This enables Kodi also to scrape metadata about the shows from the web and add same to its own databases for your use.

Now, we're off and running in building our music, movie, and TV databases.

CHAPTER 12

■ ■ ■

Backup and Updating

There is nothing permanent except change.

—Heraclitus of Ephesus

Things do change; that's for sure.

Here I sat, almost finished with this book, and Kodi comes out with an updated version; but this is good. A lot of rewriting and creation of new illustrations ensued, but that's good. Had this manuscript been turned in earlier, it would have been behind the curve. As it is, everything I've already covered is now current.

This chapter covers backup, saving a copy of Kodi in case something goes wrong and you need to step back, and the update process for newly released versions. The two topics belong together.

First, you'll learn about protecting all the arduous work you've done in configuring and adding media to your system. Hours and hours upon hours and hours.

Backup and Restore

Making a restorable copy of Kodi (called a *backup*) is reasonably fast. The rule of thumb for how often backups should be created depends on how much stuff, should your system crash, you are willing to manually restore. In my case, that means regular backups, since redoing stuff already done is boring. Besides, how can we recall all the new links and changes we'll often implement in a growing media center?

Backing Up

The Raspberry Pi/LibreELEC/Kodi combination media center hardware and software has an easy method of copying the system software and Kodi into a backup file. Let's do it now:

1. Go to System ➤ LibreELEC ➤ System.

2. Move down the menu to Create System and Kodi Backup and click it (Figure 12-1).

3. Click OK and a copy will be saved in the Backup directory on the SD card (the default location but can be changed if desired).

© Ralph Roberts 2017
R. Roberts, *Mastering Media with the Raspberry Pi*,
https://doi.org/10.1007/978-1-4842-2728-2_12

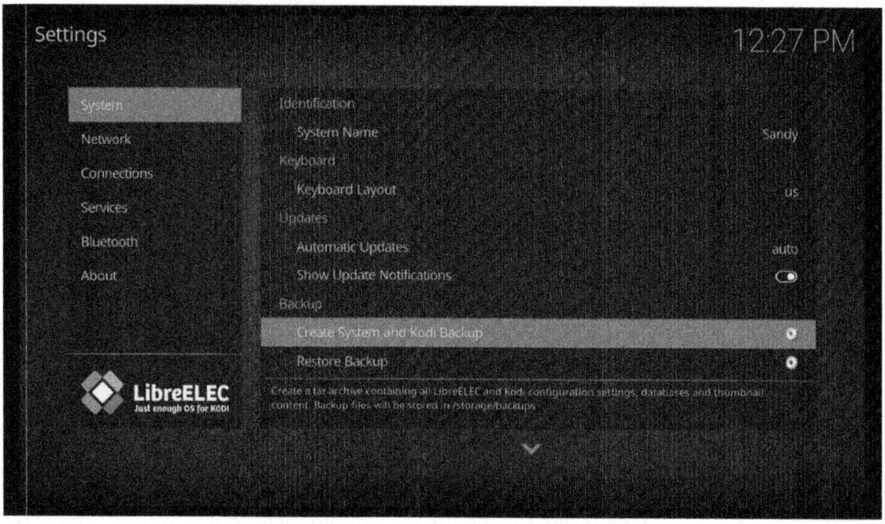

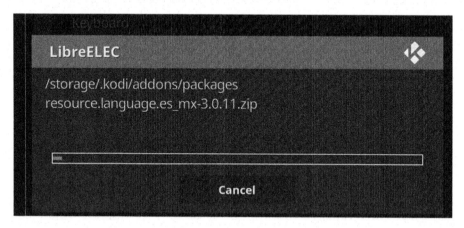

Figure 12-1. *Use* `Create System and Kodi Backup` *under LibreELEC settings to save your Kodi-based entertainment center software and configurations*

Those three steps do the job. You'll see a progress bar showing the files backing up. This process builds an archive file in the /backup directory on your microSD card but can take a long time, especially as our media centers become more and more populated with media links. Figure 12-2 shows Backup in action.

Figure 12-2. *Backing up can take time, so you might want to start it when you've finished binge-watching for the night and are ready for bed*

Since space is limited on your RPi's microSD card, a good practice is to keep only the most recent backups there (in case they're needed for restoring your files) and move the others to network or cloud storage. Having those means, for example, that if your Raspberry Pi gets swiped or fails (either hardware problem or the microSD card becomes corrupted), $35 brings you a replacement and copying a backup from the network restores all your great stuff.

I keep my copies of backups on one of my Windows computers (in fact, the very one in use for writing this book). My Raspberry/Kodi computer is on the network, so finding and copying files from the /backup directory on it is easy (it's in the root directory, the first one you see). Then, just for double safety, I upload the backup of the backup file to Google Drive, out there in the cloud. Figure 12-3 shows the system and Kodi backup file on my Windows computer. This backup file is 1.48GB, and it will only get longer. In other words, expect copying it to take time.

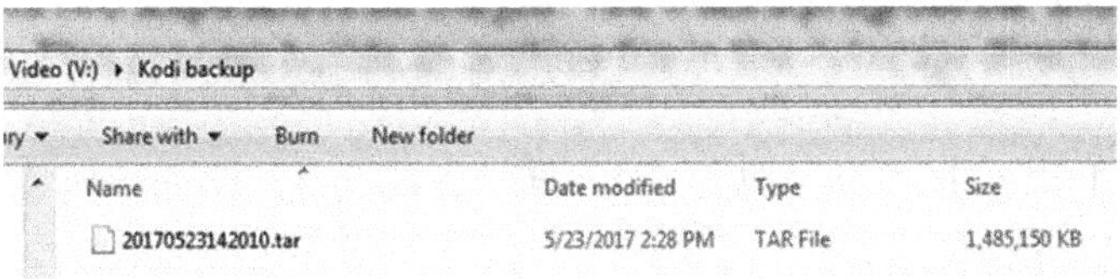
Video (V:) ▸ Kodi backup
Share with ▾
Burn
New folder
Name
Date modified
Type
Size
20170523142010.tar
5/23/2017 2:28 PM
TAR File
1,485,150 KB

Figure 12-3. *Copy of a system and Kodi backup file on a Windows computer*

The .tar extension, by the way, is a Linux compressed storage format first developed for tape archival decks; hence its name. You need not worry about the format; Kodi handles the compressing and uncompressing as necessary.

We always hope backups are never needed, but sometimes stuff happens. Uncompressing and rebuilding an RPi/LibreELEC/Kodi system is called *restoring*.

Restoring

To restore from a backup, click System ➤ LibreELEC ➤ System ➤ Restore Backup. The resulting dialog box shows the backup files in the /storage directory on the RPi's SD card. In Figure 12-4 we have two. The date is embedded in the file's title, which lets us find the most recent easily enough. Click that one to restore it, and the rest is automatic.

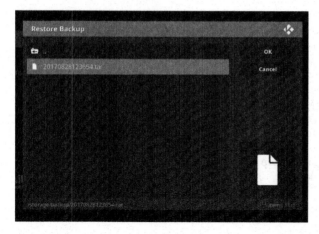

Figure 12-4. *Clicking* System ➤ LibreELEC ➤ System ➤ Restore Backup *causes Kodi to rebuild your media center with all the files and configuration you've done in past weeks, months, or years*

That procedure, of course, works fine if Kodi still runs. If you're replacing the RPi, you have extra steps but you can still get all your files back. Do the following (for a new RPi):

1. Install LibreELEC, which includes Kodi.

2. Once Kodi runs and is on your network, copy the most recent backup file you have to /storage on the RPi's SD card.

3. Now go to System ➤ LibreELEC ➤ System ➤ Restore Backup, click on the backup archive, and wait patiently as the files unpack and shuffle into place.

Now, on to updating, both minor and major—the latter of which describes the latest version of Kodi, recently released version 17.3, or Krypton. (Krypton was Superman's home planet, the one that blew up and produced Kryptonite.) The previous Kodi version, Jarvis, was 16.1.

Updating

Updating means installing new files as LibreELEC or Kodi releases them. Keeping your media center up-to-date is important for several reasons:

- Security

- Adding new features

- Fixing bugs

First, you'll find minor updates easy to set up.

Minor Updates

For minor updates, simply set LibreELEC/Kodi to update automatically. Go to System
➤ LibreELEC ➤ System (the same screen we used earlier to accomplish backups and
restores. Under Updates, the Automatic Updates selection should show Auto on the right
side of bar—if not, click once to activate it (Figure 12-5).

Figure 12-5. Turn on Automatic Updates, and minor updates stay up-to-date

Major Updates

When an updated version of Kodi comes out, a major upgrade procedure is required.
This means that LibreELEC and the other packages of operating systems with Kodi
embedded must release a new package containing both the underlying operating system
and the newer version of Kodi. We'll need to download this package (in our case, from
https://libreelec.tv/downloads) and install it on our RPi.

■ **Caution**   Before doing a major upgrade, always back up, and copy the backup file
to another computer or the cloud! Upgrades can fail, and having a backup then becomes
important to restore your system.

For a full backup, to be entirely safe if something fails, you should first accomplish
two tasks:

> **Back up all your settings and lists**: Do an archival backup
> from within Kodi (like we did earlier) and copy the .tar file to
> another computer on your network and/or the cloud.

Duplicate your microSD card: Use the WinDisk32 imager software recommended earlier in this book and use a Windows computer to copy the image from your media center SD card to an image file on the PC. Then you can write out a copy that plugs in and your current system is running again. If the upgrade crashes, you'll be glad to have this complete backup.

Reasons for Upgrading to Kodi 17.3

If you're still running an earlier version of Kodi, I recommend updating now. Kodi v17 (Krypton), the latest release being 17.3, provides many improvements in performance and ease-of of use, and a bonanza of new features. There are literally thousands of reasons to upgrade. Some of these are listed on the http://kodi.tv web site:

Update Estuary and Estouchy with some bug fixes and improvements.

Fix EDL skipping

Fix slow song smartplaylist

Several PVR fixes

Update Chorus webinterface

Fix addons not being marked broken when they are updated with broken flag

Add limiter on random songs which should prevent large memory usage on big libraries

Improve keyboard mapping during button mapping

Improve analog stick handling

Improve plugin performance when building the content list

Include RTMP inputstream add-on for Windows

Don't close subtitle stream when switching audio

Fix replaygain for music files

Fix controllers buttons on Android

Fix music cleanup hanging on large MySQL music database

Fix use of SMB on Android on new installs

Fix possible Kodi upgrade migration hang during add-on update process

Add check in Windows installer for Service Packs and updates that Kodi needs to operate

Don't try to read tags from internet audio streams

Add setting to disable controller rumble on notifications

We don't have to understand every bullet point here to see that a lot has been done. If that is not enough to get you excited about doing a major upgrade, check out a much fuller list at http://kodi.wiki/view/Kodi_v17_(Krypton)_changelog.

Bummer, Agony, and a Package Provider Change

Kodi 16.1, the version we've been using up to this point, is contained in the LibreELEC 7.01 package. The latest version of Kodi is 17.3, so we'll need a new package for our RPi platform but not necessarily LibreELEC.

I'm going to save you quite possibly several hours and a bit of mental anguish, all of which happened when I tried to upgrade to Kodi 17.3. Luckily, the image of my LibreELEC/Kodi 16.1 card allowed a full recovery from the first disastrous attempt.

It seems LibreELEC's package for the RPi still has a few problems. To be fair to those fine folks, I understand that some of the nightly releases (ongoing development) kill some of these bugs, but I wanted a stable release with all the new features.

In a nutshell, I first attempted a manual upgrade of my existing system, with its tons of music, movies, TV shows, and useful add-ons. I wanted to keep them. Had it worked, all my libraries and so forth would be on the new software. It did not work. After downloading and copying the manual upgrade .tar file over to the Upgrade folder in the old Kodi, all I got was the LibreELEC logo, and then a black screen. Googling the problem showed others having the same problem getting the new LibreELEC/Kodi 17.3 package running.

I tried a bunch of configuration changes, editing files down on the operating system, something most people would not want to do. Nothing worked.

So I decided just to download the image and build the whole danged media center from scratch again. Which I did and, short burst of excitement soon falling flat, it came up into Kodi 17.3. However, it was soon apparent, after more hours of work, that the system still had problems, two of the biggest being Samba and no sound. Again, others were fighting the same problems and I tried their tips but to no avail.

Samba is the protocol used by Kodi in communicating with other computers on local networks. I could see and access Kodi from other computers, but Kodi could not see them. A severe deficiency, that—if Kodi can't see its video and music sources on the other computers, I can't watch movies, and so on.

For sound, I use a HifiBerry Amp+, which drives my speakers nicely. It worked fine on the earlier Kodi but silence ruled on the new LibreELEC package (8.0.3). Something had to be done, and Mr. Google was consulted on other ways of getting Kodi 17.3 (Krypton) onto a Raspberry Pi.

I want what you most likely want, Kodi 17.3 but with all my changes, links, and so on. So, I refer you again to the quote at the start of this chapter, "There is nothing permanent except change." For me, it was time for a change.

What We Learned

Change can be good; that's what we learned primarily—me the hard way, you guys by example. LibreELEC is a good choice as the enabling operating system for Kodi. As an enthusiastic fan of this new fork said on the LibreELEC site, "It runs smooth as butter." Personally, I prefer butter on my popcorn and not my media center but to each his own, eh?

Now, let's get more serious. This chapter concentrated on backing up our media centers, which we should do periodically. Having a recent backup file on another computer on the network and out on the cloud somewhere, such as Dropbox or Google Drive, protects your data. Making a copy of your microSD card is also a good idea as good insurance in case the card in use gets corrupted or fails in some way.

We met minor updates; they happen automatically if you've configured them. I didn't mention add-ons, but they, too, can update themselves. Most of us will wind up with copious amounts of add-ons, the third-party apps that enhance our media center software.

CHAPTER 13

■ ■ ■

Managing Your Libraries

A library is a place where you learn what teachers were afraid to teach you.

—Alan M. Dershowitz

Several times during this book, we've added items to Kodi's libraries. The media libraries—for videos, music, and pictures—give us power databases for managing our collections of movies, TV shows, albums, songs, photos, graphics, and all the other types of media a media center should have. That's all good, but one question comes to mind—*who manages the managers?*

Kodi's libraries do not store the actual movies, music, or any other media file. Instead these databases remember links to places where files exist, what we call resources. Resources can be directories on the SD card (not the best practice; slow retrieval and limited space), hard drives attached to your Raspberry Pi (much better), drives on the local network, directories in accessible storage out in the cloud, web sites, and others.

However, in the library databases, Kodi scrapes metadata from the Internet and/or records data you enter. Titles, actors, genre, plots, music, album covers, liner copy, writers, composers, fanart, and all sorts of other information making your entertainment even more interesting. Lots of stuff.

With the introduction of Kodi 17.3, the version we've used throughout, the Kodi development team has made control and maintenance of the resource links easier to find and manage. That's what this chapter shows you.

We begin by working with video, then music, and then pictures.

Video

Once you understand that library management concerns resource link management, you'll find this part of Kodi simple and useful. We start by clicking the gear-shaped icon on the upper left of Kodi's main screen (at least in the default Estuary skin it's there). This opens the System screen as shown in Figure 13-1.

© Ralph Roberts 2017
R. Roberts, *Mastering Media with the Raspberry Pi*,
https://doi.org/10.1007/978-1-4842-2728-2_13

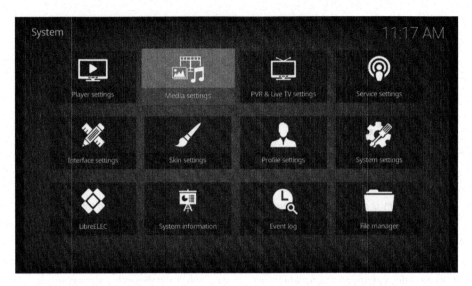

Figure 13-1. Kodi's System screen gives us access all the configuration settings

On the System screen, click Media settings. The next screen, Settings/Media, has several items. Clicking the icon in the lower left, currently shown as Standard, lets us rotate around through Basic, Standard, Advanced, and Expert levels, each added more choices. Play with that but we'll use the Standard choice in this chapter since it provides the simple maintenance options we need.

Manage Sources

Hover your cursor over Library and you'll see the screen shown in Figure 13-2.

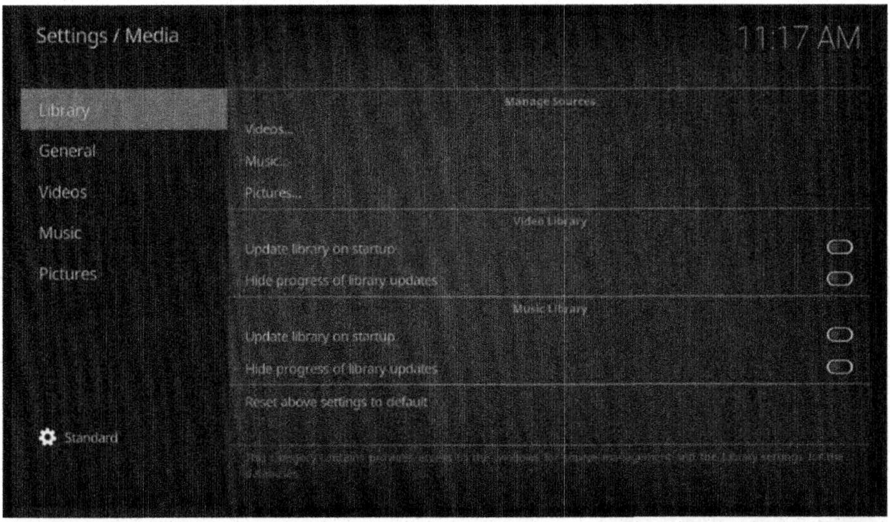

Figure 13-2. The items we need for library management

We'll refer to this screen a few times. Note the first section heading, Managing Sources. We'll look at this section for all three libraries first, and then come back to this screen for the other items on it.

Slide the cursor over to highlight Videos and click. We now get a listing of video resources, as shown in Figure 13-3. Yours will be different from mine with the exceptions of the last item, Add videos. More about it in a moment (and yes, we've certainly seen it before in setting up the resources scanned into our video library originally). The choices are here as a convenience in managing, specifically on this screen, the video library's resource links.

Figure 13-3. The list of video resources on my Kodi media center with one highlighted (selected by hovering the cursor over its title)

175

Select a resource you might want to change and right-click it. The dialog box in Figure 13-4 appears.

Figure 13-4. *Dialog box for editing a resource link*

An important point here is that you can get to this dialog box on any screen where resource titles appear. The developers just pulled them together here for ease of management tasks. Let's look at each choice in Figure 13-4.

Play: A shortcut presenting a listing of the resource's contents. Click a title to play.

Add to favorites: Add this resource to the Favorites quick access listing (the entry with a star icon next to it near the bottom of the main menu on Kodi's main screen).

Edit source: Brings up the dialog box shown in Figure 13-5. You can edit the path to the source (in the example here, it's on the 4TB drive attached to my Raspberry Pi) and/or change the title of the source. Clicking Browse lets you move the source to another directory, drive, online location, and so on. Two reasons for changing the resource's path are:

a. You've moved the resource to another location.

b. Replacing the current resource link with another.

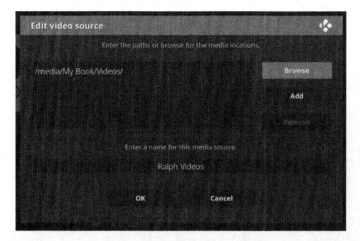

Figure 13-5. *Editing the video source link*

Remove source: Delete this source. Be careful here; this step deletes all references in the library to any title in the source directory (but not the original files).

Choose thumbnail: Add a photo or graphic for this resource, which appears whenever it's accessed. In this case, the resources are videos I've produced, so I put in my photo (Figure 13-6). You can have anything you like. It's *your* media center.

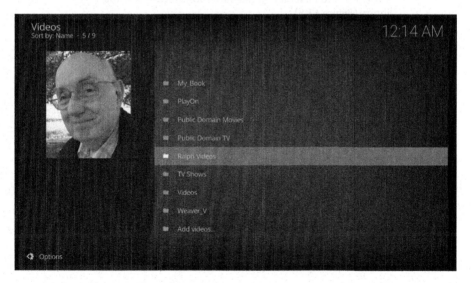

Figure 13-6. *Add a picture or other graphic to better identify the resource. For a collection of my videos, I used my picture.*

177

Set content: Configuration for the way this link works (Figure 13-7).

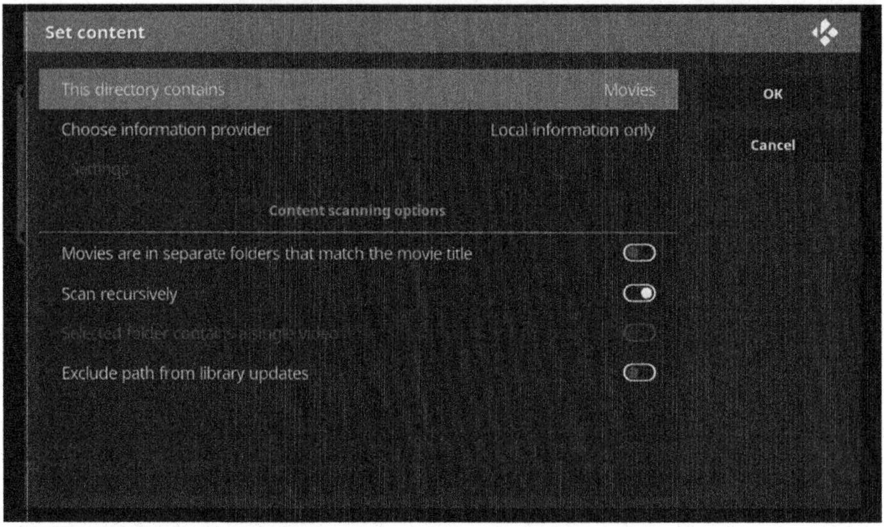

Figure 13-7. *Configure parameters concering the operation of this link.*

Scan for new content: Ask Kodi to scan for new content you've downloaded into this resource link and add it to the library (Figure 13-8).

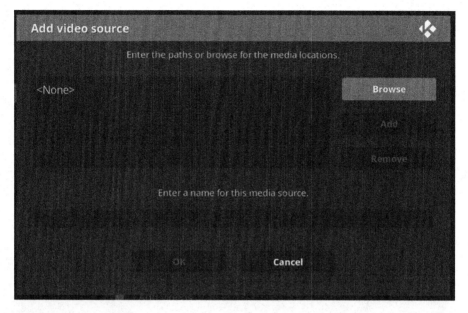

Figure 13-8. *Use this choice in scanning for new content, that is, when you've download new movies into the resource directory and want to add them to the video database*

Video Library

Referring back to Figure 13-2, the next section on the screen is entitled Video Library and offers a couple of configurations for adjusting the way our video libraries work; see them in Figure 13-9.

Figure 13-9. *Configuring how and when Kodi scans new content to the video library*

The top choice, Update library on startup, sounds reasonable. However, once you've accumulated hundreds of movies and music files, updating can take a good long time and slow your media center down. I know when I decide to turn my home theater on, flop on the couch, and look for a movie to watch, any delay is irksome. Best practice, in my opinion, is to update manually (scan for new content as described earlier and also elsewhere in this book) and do so only when you know you've downloaded new stuff. No need to scan every single time the system is powered up.

My preference on the second parameter, Hide progress of library updates, is leaving it on. I enjoy watching all that activity happening in the upper right of the screen. Your choice on your system, on or off as you like.

OK, now on to managing your music library, which is handled much the same as we did for the video library above.

Music

Taking care of resource links in your music library or making changes to them is very similar to what we learned earlier about the same operations for your video library. However, a few minor differences pop up.

On the screen shown in Figure 13-2, choose Music and you'll see the screen in Figure 13-10. Here you'll see your music resource links and using or configuring them works, as noted, much like for the video library. You can, of course, reach this same screen from within Music on Kodi's main menu and clicking the Files icon. As mentioned earlier, this section is just a convenience, pulling all the library maintenance items into one place.

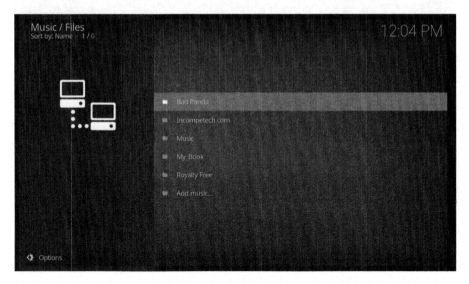

Figure 13-10. *Listing of music resource links*

Click (left-click) on any resource (I've highlighted my public domain Bad Panda music, downloaded from the Internet's archive, http://archive.org). Clicking it shows (just as in the video library section earlier) the titles in the resource (which in this case is a directory on another computer connected to my local network), as shown in Figure 13-11.

Figure 13-11. *Music files in my Bad Panda resource; just click and play*

Go back up to the Music ➤ Files screen and right-click a resource link. You'll get the dialog box in Figure 13-12, which differs slightly from the one from a video link. First, there are only six items instead of seven.

Edit source

Make default

Remove source

Choose thumbnail

Scan item to library

Add to favourites

Figure 13-12. *Right-clicking a music resource link yields a slightly different dialog box from the video one*

Missing are Play and Change Content. New is Make Default and Scan for New Content changed to Scan Item to library (but works the same. The Make default choice causes this to be the source first shown under Music. Otherwise, managing links works just like video.

Referring again to Figure 13-2, the Music Library section has the same two configuration choices on updating the library on startup and whether you want to watch it scroll through files or not. The same preferences noted earlier apply but these operate independently of those in the video section.

And, not to forget, at the bottom of the listed music resources links is the Add music link. As in videos, this is how you add new music resources.

Pictures

Once more yet again we look at Figure 13-2 and click Pictures to manage picture links to resources. Unlike video and music, the two choices on when and how checks for new content occurs are not available (Figure 13-13).

Figure 13-13. *Manage or add picture links from this screen*

Managing the links works the same way you've seen. Click on a link to list and play it. Right-click a link for the dialog box in Figure 13-14.

Figure 13-14. *Fewer choices than in video or music*

Choosing Add pictures at the bottom of the links list, as with the other two libraries, allow new links to be added to the pictures library.

What We Learned

The three library databases in Kodi work using links to resources—which can be directories on attached media, on other computers on the local network, or out on the Internet. Movies, music, picture files are not stored in the database but rather Kodi links to them. What does get stored is metadata scraped from the Internet—such as actors, plots, singers, music groups, and all sorts of other information about specific media files (if available).

This area in Kodi duplicates others under the movies, music, pictures choices from Kodi's main menu but is conveniently grouped here for when you need to perform library maintenance.

CHAPTER 14

■ ■ ■

System Management

There is only one satisfying way to boot a computer

—J.H. Goldfuss

The new default skin, Estuary, makes system configuration and other administrative tasks much easier. In Confluence, there were different paths to the various system-related submenus. In Estuary, just click the gear icon at the upper left of the main screen. The System screen that comes up has all twelve configuration menus in one handy place, which nicely simplifies finding what we need in a timely manner. Remember, this is media center software—we're here for entertainment, not to work. Any of that popcorn left?

Twelve Powerful Icons

Let's get started. Figure 14-1 shows what the System menu looks like.

Figure 14-1. *The System menu*

© Ralph Roberts 2017
R. Roberts, *Mastering Media with the Raspberry Pi*,
https://doi.org/10.1007/978-1-4842-2728-2_14

Each of the twelve icons in Figure 14-1 represents a submenu of items falling within the general category in the icon's title. For example, we can expect the Player settings icon to access a submenu with items related to the configuration of players. Indeed, that's true.

Let's look at each of these twelve configuration menus. Once we understand what they do and where to find functions needed to modify the operation of Kodi, we'll control our media center rather than letting it control us.

As we go through these configuration and other system settings, you might want to follow along on your own Kodi-powered media center. It'll help you learn these items faster and retain them longer.

Player Settings

The name gives it away; these are settings linked to controlling media players. As you see in Figure 14-2, there are six items on the Settings ➤ Player submenu. They are on the left side of the screen as shown.

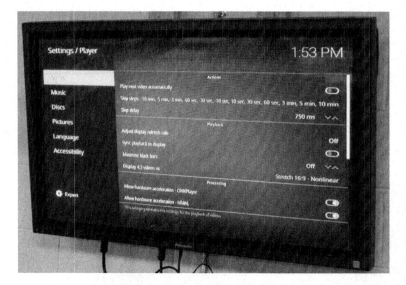

Figure 14-2. Settings ➤ Player submenu

Following is a capsule look at the submenu items shown in Figure 14-2. Select each by moving the cursor over the title and then right into the major portion of the screen, where you can now access and change configuration settings.

Before you start configuring, look at the small gear icon at the bottom left of the screen. Clicking on it rotates you through four levels of expertise—Basic, Standard, Advanced, and Expert. The one you chose determines how many configuration items appear in each category. If you don't want to be bothered by the more esoteric settings, select Basic or Standard. For the purposes of our familiarization exercise, set this selection to Expert so that you can see everything.

■ **Tip**   Notice in these configuration items that, as you move the cursor over each one, an explanation of that item's purpose appears at the bottom of your screen.

Video: Configurations for how movies and other videos are played by Kodi, it's divided into three principal areas—Actions, Playback, and Processing.

Music: Presents configuration choices controlling how music plays and is divide into two categories—Actions and Playback (again, explanation of each configuration is at the bottom of the screen).

Disc: Lets you configure the playback of discs and is divided into sections for DVD, Blu-ray, and Audio CDs.

Pictures: Primarily controls aspects of slideshows.

Language: Two areas here allow us to select the preferred language for audio and subtitles (which can be different).

Accessibility: These also configure audio and subtitles but in this case with regard for the visually impaired and the hearing impaired with settings for each.

■ **Tip**   Estuary does not have arrows at the bottom of the screen for going back up a level as Confluence does—use the Esc key on your keyboard or right-click the mouse.

Media Settings

Configuration items affecting media files, links, and so forth get selected in this submenu. There are five selections, each have several configuration choices. They are (again, when in Expert mode):

Library: Gives us three areas of configuration choices—Manage sources, Video library, and Music library.

General: Mostly concerned with how all files and directories are shown, hidden, and handled.

Video: Same as the previous but affects only video files.

Music: Configurations for music files only.

Pictures: For picture files only.

Figure 14-3 shows the Settings ➤ Media submenu.

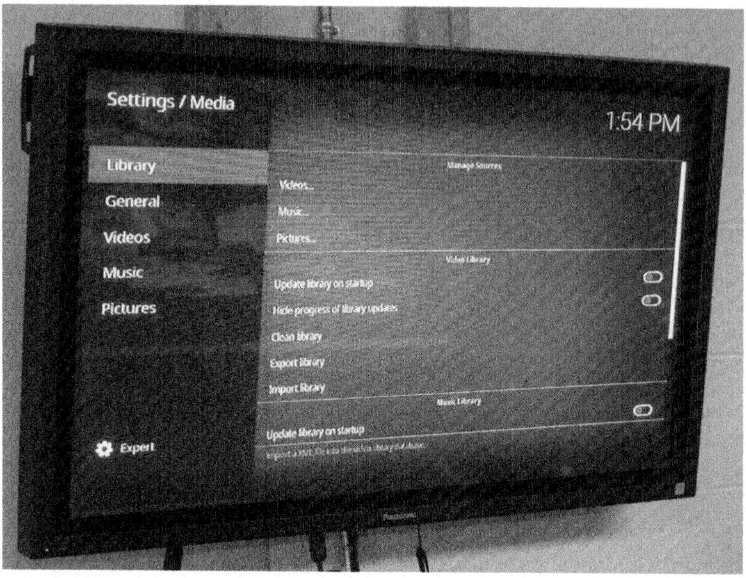

Figure 14-3. *Settings ➤ Media submenu*

PVR & Live TV Settings

PVR (Personal Video Recorder) and live (streaming) TV are covered in more detail in Chapter 16. A PVR allows you to schedule and control video recording devices to save your favorite programs or sports for later viewing. This submenu (Figure 14-4) allows configuration of devices and services related to this category.

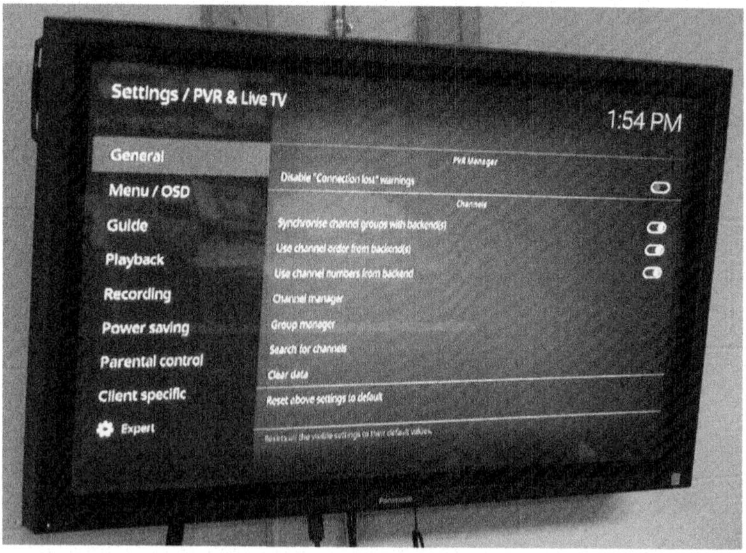

Figure 14-4. *Settings ➤ PVR & Live TV submenu*

Here's what the configuration choices on the left in Figure 14-4 do:

General: Refers to configuration for PVR managers (we'll see what those are and how to install them in Chapter 16) and channels.

Menu/OSD: Menu items and OSD (On Screen and Display) appear as a brief image overlaying the screen with information such as channel number, time, and so on, and you can control their duration and so forth via the configuration choices here.

Guide: This controls the presentation of information about upcoming show schedules.

Playback: Divided into General and RDS (Radio Data System protocol) playback configuration.

Recording: Choices for how recording is accomplished.

Power saving: Enables various modes to save power.

Parental control: Provides parents program controls to stop the kiddies from watching the naughty stuff.

Client specific: Configuration options for various PVR add-ons, these options appear here only for the add-on supports, such as

Service Settings

Services are generally processes running in the background that do things when you need them to. Processes include networking, audio routines, video player, display, and scores of others. Figure 14-5 shows the screen.

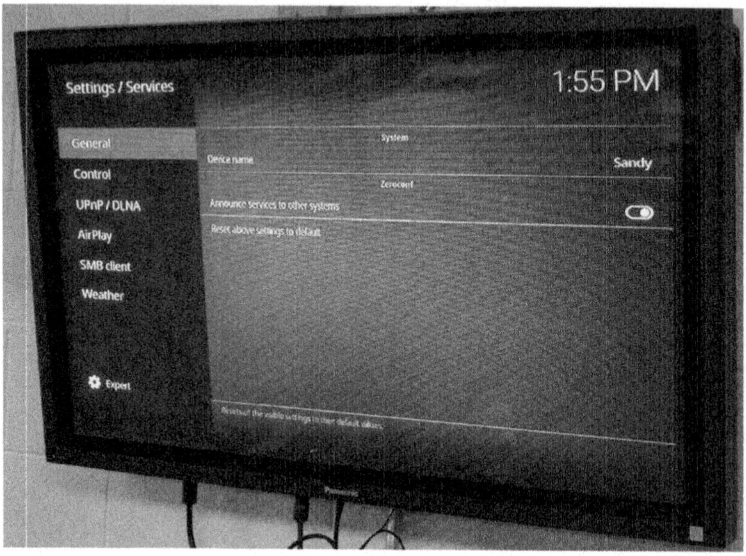

Figure 14-5. *Settings* ➤ *Services submenu*

Here are the service categories we can configure:

General: only two configurations, the name (my device is named "Sandy") and allowing the device to be seen over the network (a good thing for your local network).

Control: allow control via Kodi's built-in web interface and permit remote control by applications on the system.

UPnP/DLNA: UPnP (Universal Plug and Play) and DLNA (Digital Living Network Alliance), which are protocol for installing devices to computers, work together in allowing devices such as smartphones, personal computers, and so on to play and send media from and to Kodi, and you can configure the parameters of this here.

AirPlay: Apple's Airplay can be used to stream music and video to AirPlay-enabled devices on your home network; configure that here.

SMB client: SMB (Server Message Block) is a networking protocol supported by both Linux and Microsoft Windows— the important configuration here is making sure Kodi belongs to the same workgroup as the rest of your local network.

Weather: As you recall, in Chapter 13 I set up a weather service on my system so that when the Weather option on Estuary's main screen is clicked, it shows the weather forecast and other information—this is where I set up and activated it.

Interface Settings

Skin: This is where we switched from Estuary to Confluence in the last chapter—you can change skins here, change colors and fonts among other cosmetics.

Regional: Configure language and units of measure.

Screensaver: Choose a screensaver and specify how it works.

Master lock: Set up passcode protection, restricting the system to use only by yourself and those you authorize.

Other: Change the startup window from Home to another and set up an RSS (Really Simple Syndication) feed for the home window.

Figure 14-6 shows the Settings ➤ Interface screen.

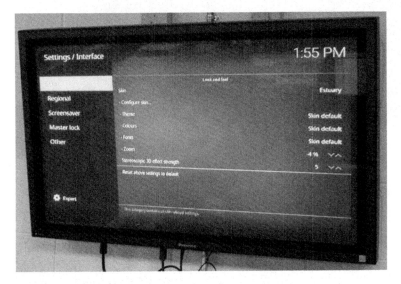

Figure 14-6. *Settings ➤ Interface submenu*

Skin Settings

The Settings ➤ Skin settings submenu (Figure 14-7) allows additional configurations of skins. There are three selections:

General: Cosmetic changes to the skin such as adding animating menus and enabling weather information, media tags, and touch mode (requires the presence of a touch screen).

Main menu items: Allows the editing or deletion of main menu (the top level menu) items.

Artwork: Change appearance by adding artwork and selecting display fonts.

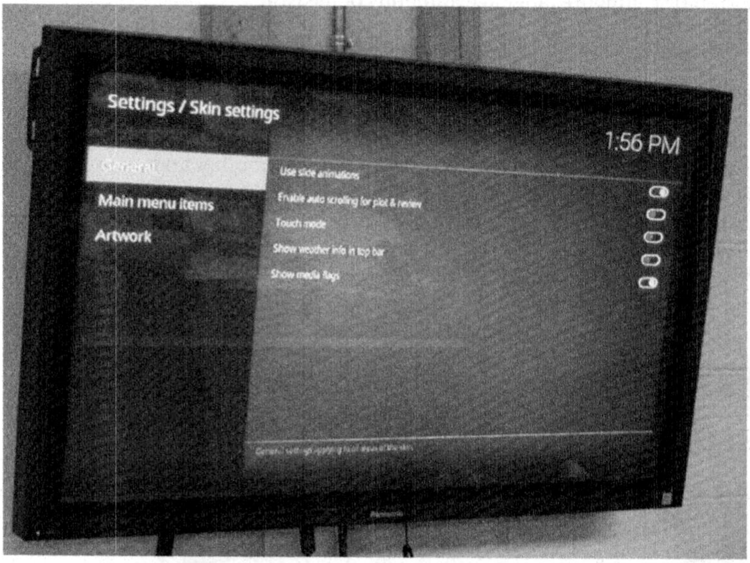

Figure 14-7. Settings ➤ Skin settings submenu

Profile Settings

The Settings ➤ Profiles screen (Figure 14-8) has two selections—General and Profiles. The first lets you configure the showing of a login screen when the system first boots. In the second you can add photos of the master user and any other users on the system.

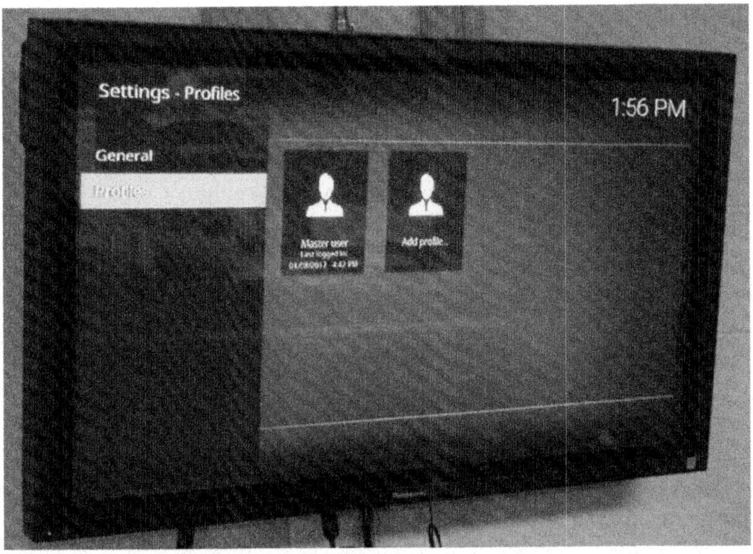

Figure 14-8. *Settings - Profiles submenu*

System Settings

The Settings ➤ System submenu (Figure 14-9) is one of the more important ones.

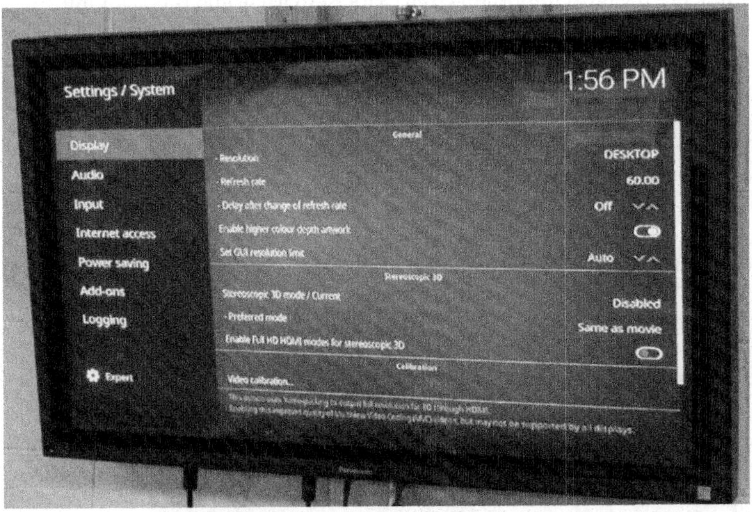

Figure 14-9. *Settings ➤ System*

The areas of configuration do the following:

Display: Configures resolution, refresh rate, and other general aspects of your screen, and there is also a section of choices for stereoscopic 3D (obtaining an apparent three-dimensional effect by traditionally wearing special glasses).

Audio: There are many choices here, including audio output device, stereo upmix, resample quality, and much more.

Input: This has two sections (Peripherals and Devices); come here to configure your mouse, touch screen support, and remote controllers.

Internet access: Set up proxy servers and limit Internet bandwidth here.

Power Saving: Additional power-saving options.

Add-ons: Configure add-ons for automatic updates, types of notifications, and so on.

Logging: Configure debugging and event logs.

LibreELEC

Like System Settings covered earlier, LibreELEC Settings (Figure 14-10) is another of the more important configuration submenus. In fact, it's my opinion, these are the two most significant. The first has the most important choices for Kodi itself, and this is for the underlying operating system.

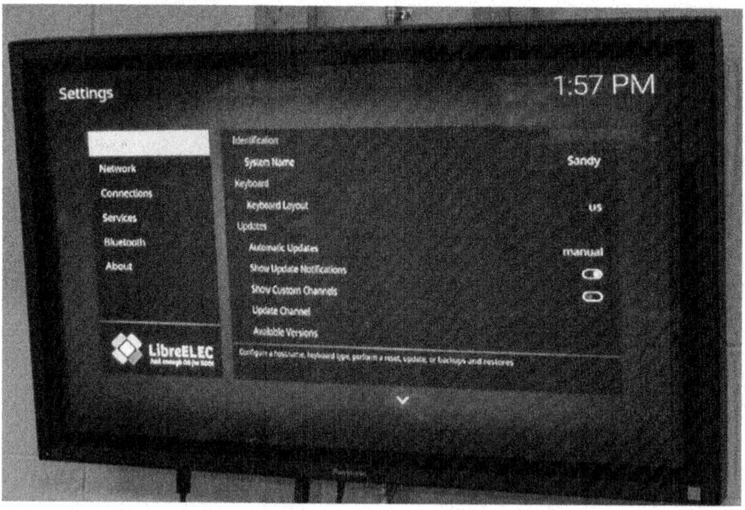

Figure 14-10. *LibreELEC Settings*

Here's what this submenu does for us:

System: System name (Sandy for mine), keyboard layout, configuring updates (I like automatic), backups (do these regularly), and restores.

Network: Wireless networks, wired networks, turn your system on as an access point, setup timeservers—all this and more.

Connections: Choose and connect to wireless access points.

Services: Configure SSH, Samba, Bluetooth, Cron and more.

Bluetooth: Once Bluetooth has been enabled in Services, configure it here.

About: Not configuration but rather an information screen about this LibreELEC package (8.02).

System Information

Shown in Figure 14-11, this is an information screen about the current version of Kodi.

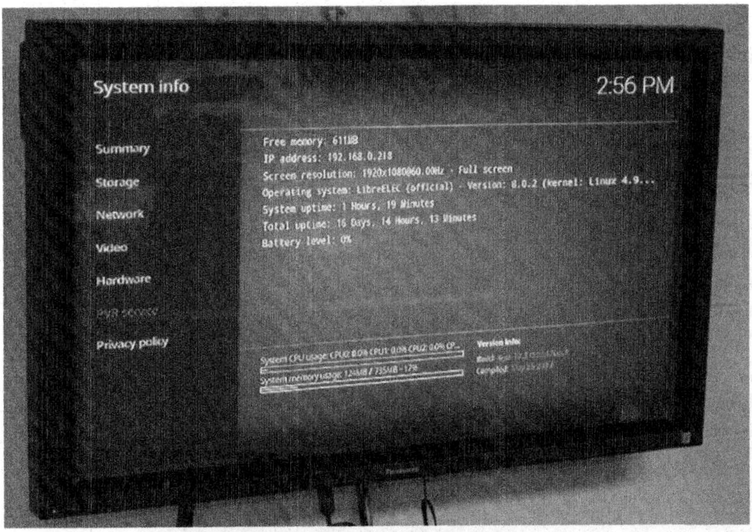

Figure 14-11. System info submenu

Event Log

A log of events, useful in troubleshooting. Not much in mine; just the last boot (Figure 14-12).

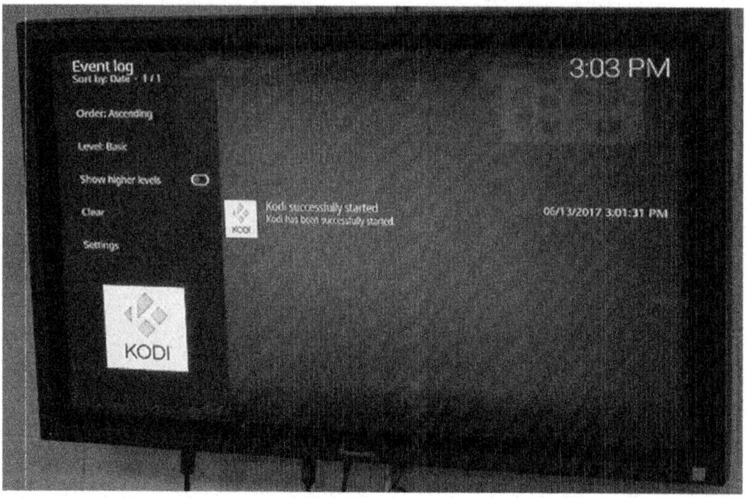

Figure 14-12. Event log submenu

File Manager

A file management utility. In Figure 14-13 I've opened my ham radio photographs picture resource, which is on another computer on my network.

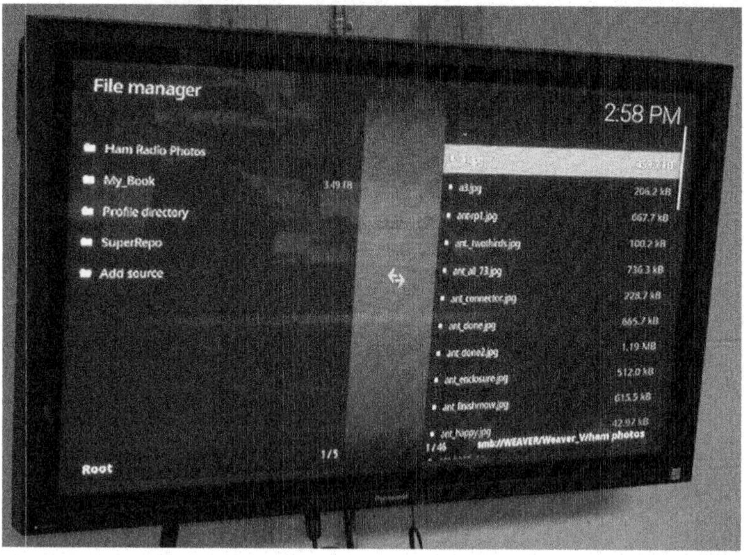

Figure 14-13. File manager submenu

To use the file manager, right-click the name of a file. A dialog box appears with the following operations available:

- `Select all`
- `Add to favorites`
- `Rename`
- `Delete`
- `Make new folder`
- `Switch media`

The last operation, `Switch Media`, allows us to retag the file as movie, music, or picture.

What We Learned

In this chapter, we have explored the Settings menu and its submenus, the twelve powerful icons. We've found that Estuary gives us all those important configuration submenus in one handy place. The two most important ones are System Settings and LibreELEC Settings.

Now, let's add some add-ons and enhance our media centers. Coming up, just the turn of the page away.

CHAPTER 15

■ ■ ■

Adding Add-Ons

Life is too short to run proprietary software.

—Bdale Garbee

Add-ons consist of small programs designed to add extra features, services, and capabilities to Kodi. Thousands already exist. More are being created pretty much daily. Third parties (groups or individuals unrelated to the Kodi developers) create these add-ons. Most are not supported by the Kodi folks.

Add-ons fall into several categories, which you will learn how to use in selecting downloads in the "Download Add-ons" section later in this chapter. Here's a list to give you an idea of finding add-ons for your system (presented in the order they appear on the Download add-ons submenu)).

> Information providers: Add-ons providing information about music, albums, artists, movies, TV shows, and so on (we met some of these while learning the use of scrapers).

> Look and feel: These affect the look and operation of Kodi and include screensavers, visualization (think pretty backgrounds for your music), sounds, graphic user interfaces (GUI), skins, languages, and image collections.

> Game add-ons: A large offering of add-ons related to games, both specific and in general.

> PVR clients: Add-ons allowing Kodi to work in conjunction with various video recording devices to schedule and record video.

> VideoPlayer InputStream: Extensive list of repositories related to streaming video.

> Weather: Various add-ons forecasting and reporting weather, thus saving you from having to look out the window.

> Subtitles: Tons of add-ons displaying or managing subtitles in movies, TV shows, and other videos.

© Ralph Roberts 2017
R. Roberts, *Mastering Media with the Raspberry Pi*,
https://doi.org/10.1007/978-1-4842-2728-2_15

Lyrics : These add-ons find lyrics for songs, and many can add the lyrics to the metadata in your music library.

Add-on repository: Hundreds, probably thousands of add-on repositories for Kodi live out there in the cloud, this menu selection lists bunches of them.

Web Interface: A few add-ons allowing interaction with the web and/or your movies, music, and so on, including Kodi's own PTVL.

Services: Small programs running in the background of your system; there are many hundreds of them to choose from.

Audio encoders: Add-ons for encoding audio formations such as FLAC, MP3, and WAV.

Context menus: A double handful of add-ons, which provide popup help and other information at appropriate places.

Audio decoders: These convert all sorts of weird audio formats into something playable by Kodi.

Video add-ons: A zillion and three (or at least a lot) of video-related add-ons.

Music add-ons: The same as above except for music.

Picture add-ons: Ditto for photos and other graphics.

Program add-ons: Many, many add-ons enabling additional features in Kodi.

All exciting … but …

Here's the reality of add-ons. The pros include all those extra features, things we want, things we need, and things we gotta have. The cons? Well, there's no consistency in the quality. Some add-ons are programmed by passionate programmers working hard and without pay to give us the very best add-ons possible. Treasure those when you find them. Others come from people more passionate than programmer.

Basically, don't be surprised if you download an add-on and it doesn't work. That happens a lot. These add-ons might work fine on a PC or Mac but the guy didn't bother checking the Raspberry Pi, and it locks or just generates error messages. Or, it might have worked fine on an older version of Kodi but version 17 causes it to do a virtual meltdown. Just uninstall it and find another that provides whatever it is you want. Plenty available.

So, the following is an overview of finding, managing, and installing the various classes of add-ons for Kodi.

■ **Tip**　Lots of websites out there rate Kodi add-ons and provide lists of best apps, and reviews and/or ways of making specific add-ons work. Google, as always, is your friend (or Bing or whatever search engine you favor).

Enhancing Kodi with Add-ons

First off, add-ons are easier in Estuary. Instead of having to hunt for the add-on submenus—they were in separate places for video, music, pictures, and programs in Confluence. Estuary presents an Add-on combination submenu on its main menu screen. All major selections are right there for fast access. Figure 15-1 shows what that screen looks like when you move the cursor over its selection in Estuary. Please note that if you have a new installation of Estuary, it will not have all the add-ons shown here; this is my personal system, and I (as you likely will) keep adding goodies.

Figure 15-1. *It's now easier to find your add-ons from the main menu*

My system has many add-ons already installed, so there are thumbnails available. Also, please do not assume that because you see an add-on on my system, it's a recommendation. Not so; some of these do not work and I'm looking for replacements. A good media center should always be a work in progress.

Video Add-ons

Before we do anything to Add-ons, other than highlight it, look at the screen as depicted in Figure 15-1. This is a shortcut screen. It's showing add-ons installed on your system. Click any of the thumbnails to run that add-on or right-click to get information about it or access its settings.

Managing and Running Add-ons from Estuary's Main Screen

Like many of the screens we saw in the last chapter, this listing is also divided into sections. More sections, in fact, than the screen can show, and more thumbnails than fit on the visible part of each row. Using a mouse, you can navigate through all the listings, especially if your mouse has a scroll wheel between the two buttons.

Move the cursor into any row and move the wheel. The row scrolls horizontally, back and forth. Move the cursor to the bottom or top of the screen, and the thumbnails and icons scroll vertically.

Now, check out the top section, it's labeled Category and consists of icons, which are shortcuts to various functions. The first one (left to right), for example, is My add-ons, which takes you to that selection of the Add-ons submenu. We'll get to it shortly.

The next, Available updates, returns a list of add-ons having updates which have not been installed yet. Many add-ons can be configured to automatically update, cutting down on your maintenance tasks. Again, this is an entertainment center, so we want to max the time being entertained and decrease work whenever possible.

Next to that is Recently updated, which yields a list of add-ons now up-to-date. Then we have Install from repository. Repositories are places on the net having add-ons you can download and install. There are lots of repositories. Click this icon and explore the list.

Finally, all the way over on the right we have Search. This icon may be off your screen, so do a horizontal scroll and bring it into view. Enter a string and it searches available add-ons and returns a list. You can click on any of these for more information about it and/or install it.

Let's move on.

The Add-ons Screen

Click Add-ons on the main menu, and the Add-ons screen (Figure 15-2) appears.

Figure 15-2. *The first section on the Add-ons submenu are video add-ons*

The thumbnails shown here are all video add-ons. Click to run, or right-click for information or to change settings. This screen has a scroll bar on the right for vertical scrolling.

Click the title of this section, Video add-ons, and the screen in Figure 15-3 appears, a list of all the video add-ons installed on your systems. Again, click to run, right-click for information or to change settings.

Figure 15-3. *The Videos ➤ Add-ons submenu shows a list of your installed video-related add-ons—click an add-on's title and you can configure or uninstall it*

And, just to remind you, Options at the bottom left of the screen brings up the side menu for sorting and other useful tasks.

Now, go back up one screen. You can hit Esc on the keyboard or right-click at the top of the screen to move back. Once you're there, move the cursor over Music Add-ons.

Music Add-ons

This works the same for us as did the videos add-on thumbnails with, of course all the icons being music-related. Once more, click to run, right-click for information or to change settings. This will be true for the rest of this chapter.

Here, also, we have a scroll bar to let us check all the thumbnails. Scrolling with the mouse wheel works as well.

Figure 15-4 shows the Add-ons screen with Music add-ons highlighted.

Figure 15-4. *The second section on the Add-ons submenu shows music add-ons*

Clicking Music Add-ons, as with the video selection, gives us a list of our music add-ons, as shown in Figure 15-5.

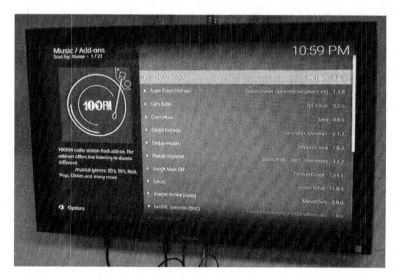

Figure 15-5. *The list of music add-ons on the system*

Program Add-ons

Program add-ons add features to the system or change the way it operates instead of providing media content. Otherwise, it works in the same pattern as video, music, and pictures (which follows):

1. Place the cursor over the selection on the Add-ons screen (see Figure 15-4) to get shortcuts to that category of add-ons.

2. Click the selection to get a listing of the add-ons in that category, like the list for programs in Figure 15-6.

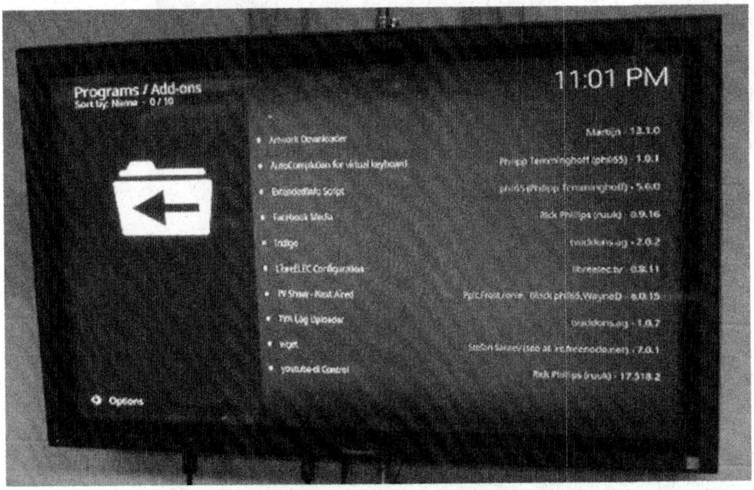

Figure 15-6. *A list of program add-ons*

Picture-Add-ons

The picture-related add-on category works just like the previous four. Figure 15-7 shows how it looks with a few picture add-ons installed.

Figure 15-7. *shortcuts for picture add-ons*

My Add-ons

Now we come to the place with the most tools for managing add-ons, My add-ons. Recall our pattern, please. Placing the cursor over the selection title causes the modification to the existing screen shown in Figure 15-8, but is not a new screen.

Figure 15-8. *Tools in My add-ons*

There are twelve of these tools. I'm not going to explain them all but suggest you play with them. That's the best way to become familiar and know where the right tool for the job (in this case managing add-ons) when you see a need for it.

Primarily this selection is for managing add-ons you already have. The next, Downloads, is for finding and installing new add-ons.

Download Add-ons

Here we can download and install add-ons; Figure 15-9 shows the shortcut display.

Figure 15-9. *The shortcuts for Download*

Figure 15-10 is the screen for browsing and selecting video add-ons. You can get information about the add-on and install it if you like. Also, don't forget to Google the add-on to see how it works for other people, especially those of us who have Raspberry Pi media centers.

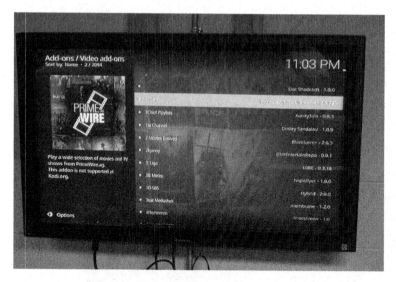

Figure 15-10. Browsing video add-ons in the Download section

What We Learned

In this chapter, we became familiar with the new, centralized layout of finding, installing, and managing add-ons. We found that all the media sections—video, music, programs, and pictures—as well as the management sections My add-ons and Downloads all operate in the same pattern: a shortcuts display, a click to get the listing, and then click to run, right-click for information or to change settings for any add-on in the list.

Now, want to watch movies and TV shows by streaming them from Netflix, Amazon, Hulu, and other providers? Of course, you do; I do. Want to have a few gazillion channels of live TV and live radio? Of course, you do; I do. All that and more coming up in the next chapter.

CHAPTER 16

■ ■ ■

Live TV, Netflix, Amazon, the Universe!

Television is a medium because anything well done is rare.

—Fred Allan

All the media listed in the title and the entire live and watch-on-demand universe of available media require *streaming*.

Why?

Because you can't store every episode of eighteen million TV series and a galaxy-full of movies on a single 32MB microSD card. Nor the complete song catalogs of Elvis, Adele, Wolfgang Amadeus Mozart, and Iris Dement (my favorite female singer) on the same card.

I know. I've tried.

Streaming audio and/or video is the answer. It lets you watch all night, all day, year-round without every running out of storage space.

Streaming

To *stream* media means it is being continuously watched or listen to by the end-user at the same time a provider's server sends it out. There's usually a buffer of a few seconds or so, and that's the only thing on your device. Just those constantly changing few seconds, which all goes away after the movie or song or other media ends.

A good analogy would be you standing on the banks of a pleasant stream in the middle of a green forest (it doesn't matter where, but staging counts). Hold up your hands and look between them at the stream as it flows by. Between your hands, you see only a small portion of the stream, but water in motion for miles slides through your field of view, constantly changing but letting view the river like a film streaming in from the Internet, a little at a time.

In short, streaming is the way media content is delivered, with only a small portion of it on your computer at any one time. Downloading the entire file is the other way, but an HD feature-length movie requires several gigabytes of disk space and stays there until you delete it.

© Ralph Roberts 2017
R. Roberts, *Mastering Media with the Raspberry Pi*,
https://doi.org/10.1007/978-1-4842-2728-2_16

For general entertainment watching, streaming is the best answer. For the movies you collect, you can always buy extra hard drives.

On Kodi, it's easy to get streaming sources. Taking movies and TV shows as an example, hundreds of video add-on exist. Some offer you large collections of streaming movies and complete TV series.

Much of the time I've spent in writing this book, I've had a music add-on, Calm Radio, streaming to me soothing and concentration-enhancing music in the background. This add-on is free if you don't mind the occasional advertisement. Or you can subscribe for uninterrupted music. It has many genres of music available. In Figure 16-1, I listen to some Indian classical music.

Figure 16-1. *The screen changes as the music does with art and information added*

Many of these add-ons offer free content, but a respectable number also want to be paid for their entertainment, especially for copyrighted movies and music, either directly or indirectly. Figure 16-2 shows an example of the latter. This add-on to allow viewing of Amazon Prime movies is free, but you must be a Prime member to watch. (Luckily, I am, because I want to watch this Star Trek movie. But not until this book is finished, eh?)

Figure 16-2. *You can find add-ons that legally stream recent movies and music, but most often have to pay for the privilege*

The streaming we've discussed so far falls under a term falling out of fashion these days, VOD or Video on Demand. In fact, the word "streaming" has essentially replaced it.

Now live television would be what? Yes, *live*. Live streams are now common, from individuals posting on YouTube and Facebook up to "big media" networks like ABC, NBC, CBS, and Fox adding streams for those who prefer the Internet to regular TV channels.

Live TV and PVR

Live streaming takes a bit more effort to achieve with your Kodi-run intelligent media center but is well worth the effort. You can get all the big-name channels and hundreds more. There are all kinds of video on demand, and you can record whatever you'd like to keep. PVR means Personal Video Recorder, and that's what you would use.

By the way, this wealth of entertaining video and music streaming, added to our onsite movie and music collections, means we can achieve, at least in my case, a long-time dream. Dump cable! Don't need it no more. No! By using IP-based TV over the Internet instead of cable or a satellite dish, my Raspberry Pi/LibreELEC/Kodi system not only gives me a huge amount of additional content, with more control over everything, and overall increased entertainment potential, but it's *cheaper*!

That's great, but you may want to use your existing cable or even broadcast signals. All that can be done for very little additional money and we look at many of ways to achieve it shortly.

Now, here's how you get live TV under Kodi's super supervision.

Live TV and PVR

Let's get our terminology right. Yes, we can get TV news and other shows streaming via the Internet as it happens. However, the definition of live TV generally accepted by the developers of Kodi and others is the traditional broadcast via digital TV or radio for voice and music. This normally arrives to you via cable or satellite antenna (and less and less these days through the air from a local broadcast TV station). That's what this section concerns. In the next one, we'll dispense with cable, satellite, and outside antennas in favor of TV over the Internet or IPTV (Internet Protocol Television).

A home theater/media center usually starts with and is built around a TV set. The end goal should be total control of that TV. To do that with Kodi, you need to control what's coming into the TV—the live digital stream of television programming.

In the beginning the TV, receiving its channels via cable or satellite disk, acts independently of Kodi. To complete the system, we'll help Kodi have the tool it needs to take command of the TV digital signal. To accomplish this, we need two parts, a *back-end* and a *front-end*. Kodi, through an add-on, provides the front-end, the graphic user interface allowing you to control channels and all the other parameters of the incoming TV signal.

As defined in the Wikipedia, the back-end is a physical device, usually a tuner box, that the Kodi front-end controls. You hook a cable or satellite digital TV to the tuner box and it breaks the signal down for Kodi to pull discrete channels from it. Here's how the Kodi developers describe it at http://kodi.wiki/view/PVR.

The PVR backend (as the server side part), which directly communicates with a TV tuner adapter(s) to receive the Live TV signals and create a video or audio stream, and record to files

The PVR client (as an add-on for Kodi)—a Kodi addon which acts as a middleware which translates the commands and controls the presentation of content from the backend to the frontend

The PVR frontend (as the Kodi graphical user interface) - Kodi that acts as a unified frontend and common interface which displays the content from all connected PVR backends

Now, the question is, which tuner box do you need and where do you get the Kodi add-on? Scores, probably hundreds of choices exist. One starting point would be on the OpenELEC site (these should work with LibreELEC also). Look at http://wiki.openelec.tv/index.php/Supported_TV_Tuners. Figure 16-3 shows some of the many inexpensive USB dongle-type tuners as sold on online sites such as Amazon.

However, don't just open Amazon and order one of these. This is just part of the back-end (back-end software also needed). You'll want to first find a good add-on and decide on the tuner based on that. To look at available PVR clients, go to Addons ➤ Downloads ➤ PVR Clients. The listing looks like Figure 16-3.

Figure 16-3. *There's a good selection of PVR clients in the default repository and more in other repositories*

If you like any of those solutions, before buying the hardware, try installing the add-on. Third-party add-ons are not always maintained and sometimes do not work. That's just the reality of noncommercial add-ons—some are great, some not so much.

Online streaming and associated software evolves even as we read this. The best tip I can give you is to use Google or other web search engines. Look for recent reviews of and articles detailing how others are solving handling streaming media, specifically for Kodi running on the Raspberry Pi. This saves you from headaches, wasted time and lets you do what the purpose of this entire book concerns, watching and listening to your media center.

Back to devices. One example is the HDHomeRun box. Look at it by searching on Amazon. It runs around $100 and works for both OTA (over the air broadcasts) or from input from a digital cable provider (of course, you'll have to keep cable and continue paying for it). You'll find an add-on in the default repository for HDHomeRun, shown in Figure 16-4.

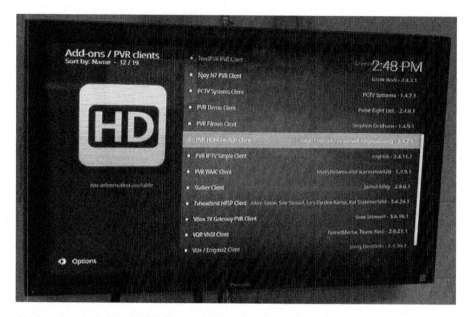

Figure 16-4. Install the HD HomeRun add-on here

Also, this is not the solution I chose—because my goal is to dump cable, and IPTV is the answer there, the ability to record shows (PVR) certainly is a worthwhile capability. There are PVRs that work with IPTV, so I'll be evaluating those.

Meanwhile, one final tip on installing PVR clients. Remember, these are just the front-ends for both watching live TV and/or recording it. You'll need the back-end software also. Check Systems ➤ PVR & Live TV for client-specific configurations. Most of these setups will have tutorials available on the Web for installation and configuring.

It takes a little effort in pulling together a PVR and Live TV installation but is relatively easy. A good starting point for more information is http://kodi.wiki/view/PVR.

Live TV from the Internet

As stated earlier, one of my goals for my Raspberry Pi/LibreELEC/Kodi media center was replacing cable and broadcast entirely by implementing IPTV or TV over the Internet. I'm happy to report that objective achieved.

Several options exist for adding IPTV to Kodi. Overall, it's easier than getting PVR and Live TV clients and back-ends working and, of course, you don't need cable or any sort of antenna. Hundreds of channels, movies, TV series, and much more come to us over the Internet.

It's simple enough to find and install IPTV for Kodi. The web site https://www. bestvpnprovider.com/best-kodi-iptv/ delivers some recommendations for both free and paid sources for IPTV providers whose services have add-ons for Kodi. Unlike in the previous section, no back-end is needed. You can have the service installed and be watching live TV, movies, or binge-watching series in minutes.

Out of the listed free services, I installed Goodfellas. Find out how to get the add-on and do the simple configuration in this YouTube video, https://www.youtube.com/watch?v=J0c8TV-o4nw. It works fine. Figure 16-5 shows what my screen looks like.

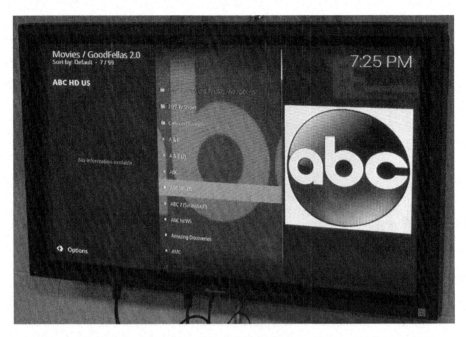

Figure 16-5. *ABC network live TV in HD via Goodfellas*

Free TV and recent movies sure is nice, but there are drawbacks as well. Many of these free IPTV providers simply collect links from others. This brings into question legalities. Links tend to disappear or not be available as copyright holders or, most likely, their attorneys squash the link. Still, there are lots of legitimate free TV in services like this one. The Goodfellas add-on seems well-supported and has been updated for Kodi 17+, but be on the lookout for copyright infringements in any add-on. Getting all seven seasons of "Game of Thrones" free is obviously too good to be true.

To rest easy on the questions of copyright infringement and obtain a better level of service, several paid IPTV providers are supported by Kodi add-ons. The one I chose was PlayOn (http://PlayOn.TV). The cost is less than cable and looks to have a lot more than my basic cable package did. Figure 16-6 shows PlayOn running on my Kodi entertainment center.

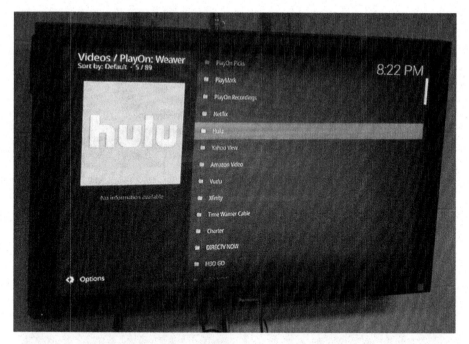

Figure 16-6. Running PlayOn IPTV on Kodi 17.3

Two more advantages of PlayOn over the free IPTVs are its built-in digital recording and the ability to cast to other devices on your network such as a smartphone, laptop, or pad. You'll also have access to Netflix, Hulu, Amazon Prime, and many other premium services, but those are not free, you'll need a logon. Still, it gives you all the entertainment you want in one place, all controlled by Kodi.

What We Learned

In this chapter, we found out about Live TV and PVR for use especially if you want to tie your existing cable or satellite TV into your entertainment center in such a way that Kodi can control it. We also discussed and looked at examples of both free and paid Internet TV (IPTV).

CHAPTER 17

■ ■ ■

Conclusions and the Future

The secret to writing a book is starting on page one and not stopping until you write the words "The End."

—Brian Koepke

Always happy to *finish* a book, and the quote above seemed appropriate for this final chapter. ... But ... No, it's not. Not appropriate for any computer book and certainly not for a book about Kodi or LibreELEC or OpenELEC and for gee whiz sure not even close for one about the Raspberry Pi.

Any book about computer software and hardware usually starts in the middle, goes along for a way, and stops before the end. It's a simple thing; no one publishes a book about something that's not yet proven and has no base of users. Once items like the Raspberry Pi and Kodi become successful, interest builds. Books and articles about them in are demand. Yet because of the complex nature of these things, they do not remain static. Development continues, features get added, improvements abound.

In a book such as this, I've presented a snapshot of where the computer and hardware is at this given moment in history. Good computer book writers don't try to explain every little detail—for those change—but rather to give you an understanding and, more importantly, a *feel* for the software and/or hardware we write about; we also attempt to anticipate and answer your questions. We strive to show you the bigger picture so that in each new release, you'll know how to get around and get your work done. Or, in this case, keep the entertainment rolling.

The Future

You can count on change. That's what successful software and hardware does, it evolves. New releases of the Raspberry Pi will have greater computer power, be faster, and have more memory. Most likely, you'll be able to add one to your home theater system by unplugging the old one, plugging in the new one, and switching the microSD card over. Things will be better.

New versions of Kodi will come out. In fact, development on Kodi 18 proceeds as you read this (see `https://kodi.tv/article/kodi-v18-windows-64-bit-here`) for additional details. The emphasis in this version is bringing Kodi from the older 32-bit to newer and more powerful 64-bit computing. No problem. The Raspberry Pi already runs 64-bit software. Yes, things will be better.

© Ralph Roberts 2017
R. Roberts, *Mastering Media with the Raspberry Pi*,
https://doi.org/10.1007/978-1-4842-2728-2_17

Enjoy the ride. You now have the basis to take advantage of every new advance in both the software and hardware of your very flexible media center.

Conclusion

The ultimate thoughts about the combination of Raspberry Pi and Kodi are short and sweet.

You can't lose using RPi as an embedded, smart controller for media centers. At only $35 suggested retail and with its powerful System on a Chip, the Raspberry Pi has plenty of power to handle the job.

Kodi has its pros and cons. I'll simplify them for you.

> Pros: Free, open source software, runs fine on the Raspberry Pi, easy to maintain and update, more features than any other media software I've found so far.

> Cons: The third-party add-ons are a pain, truly fantastic ones mixed in with ones no longer maintained and poorly programmed to begin with—Google for reviews and try them out on your system; you'll find the good ones.

Now, the votes have been cast and the final judgement here. Hold out both your hands palms up. Let the left rise rapidly and the right zoom down. Yes! The pros outweigh the cons. Kodi has so many good things we should be more than willing to put up with the add-ons. After all, there are thousands of them out there and new ones coming often. Find the good ones, uninstall the bad ones.

Apple pie and ice cream, ham and eggs, Raspberry Pi and Kodi—some things just go together well.

Thank you for reading this book and I hope it serves you as a continuing reference. Meanwhile, I'm off to binge watch "Game of Thrones" now that my work here is done. All the best!

—Ralph Roberts

The author enjoying his Raspberry Pi / LibreELEC / Kodi media center

Index

A

Add-ons, Kodi
    add-on repository, 200
    audio decoders, 200
    audio encoders, 200
    context menus, 200
    download, 207
    game, 199
    information providers, 199
    look and feel, 199
    lyrics, 200
    music, 200, 203
    My add-ons, 206
    picture, 200, 205
    program, 200, 205
    PVR clients, 199
    services, 200
    subtitles, 199
    video, 200–201
    VideoPlayer InputStream, 199
    weather, 199
    web interface, 200

B

Backup and restore, 165
Broadcom system, 6

C

Consumer Electronics Control (CEC), 79
    game controller, 81
    in Kodi, 79
    manufacturers, 80

D

Digital Millennium Copyright Act
    (DMCA), 128

E, F

Extensible Markup Language (XML), 155

G

General Purpose Input/Output
    (GPIO) pins, 84

H, I, J

High Definition Multimedia Interface
    (HDMI), 78

K

Kodi
    features, 85
        movies and media, 89
        music, 87
        UPnP, 92
    overview, 85
    purposes, 86
Kodi optimization
    Avahi (Zeroconf), 73
    bluetooth, 73
    configuration menu, 69
    Cron, 73
    drivers, 73
    facts, 65

© Ralph Roberts 2017
R. Roberts, *Mastering Media with the Raspberry Pi*,
https://doi.org/10.1007/978-1-4842-2728-2

Get the eBook for only $5!

Why limit yourself?

With most of our titles available in both PDF and ePUB format, you can access your content wherever and however you wish—on your PC, phone, tablet, or reader.

Since you've purchased this print book, we are happy to offer you the eBook for just $5.

To learn more, go to http://www.apress.com/companion or contact support@apress.com.

Apress®

CPSIA information can be obtained
at www.ICGtesting.com
Printed in the USA
LVOW13s2340021117

554833LV00003B/32/P